Infidelity or Reality

Vol. II

Bridging The Gaps…

Sweta Leena Panda

Copyright © <2024> <Sweta Leena Panda>

Dedication

To every reader holding this book, you will be loved and respected and are not left to fend for yourself. This book is a tribute to all those whose hearts have been broken through betrayal but who have the strength to look for forgiveness and regain faith. To those who are unsure of the strength of love in a time filled with chaos and people who are still holding onto a few fragments of optimism, may these words bring clarity and rebirth. For those who hold on to the idea of an eternal partnership and those who are looking to prove the strength of love, this is the perfect book for you. This journey will serve as an ally, reminding you that love is possible and the love of your life, in its purest form, can be worth the effort.

Contents

Foreword

In the quiet time of contemplation, it is common to look at what it is that keeps love going. Is it sharing desires, love, or a constant commitment? In this world where the affection we feel for one another is fragile, it's hard to understand the fragility of love, and its capacity to heal. This book gives you the chance to examine these questions through a spirit of bravery and understanding.

The issue of infidelity is not just subject to guilt and sorrow, it's beyond a question of trust. It's also an expression of the most profound emotional pain and insanity. This book contains stories of grief, but they also share tales of redemption. These aren't a form of criticism, but they can help to illuminate.

This is the manual for exploring love through all of its complexities. It reveals the secrets of connection and helps you recognize the subtle signals that call for focus and discover the possibility of a future even when it appears unattainable. If you're trying to improve your relationship or get a greater understanding of the intricate interactions between humans, this book will help you.

Name: Sweta Leena Panda

Date: 02.12.2024

Preface

In an era when relationships seem fleeting and choices limitless, the integrity and sanctity of relationships are being put under pressure. Modern temptations have weakened the once-sacred love. Infidelity can be painful, but it's not always physical. Infidelity can result from abuse, neglect, or other unresolved problems.

This book is a practical guide to understanding trust and nurturing it in your relationships. It explores the causes of infidelity, including behaviours, patterns, and societal pressures. It's not just about understanding why love ends but also about reigniting hope for its revival. Each chapter is an opportunity to build trust and a testament to the resilience of genuine connection.

As you browse through these pages, you will not only discover new perspectives and healing insights but also find the courage you need to face and overcome relationship challenges. The book is a source of strength, empowering you to confront your issues head-on.

"Love is not sustained by perfection but by the unwavering commitment to stay through imperfections."

Author: Sweta Leena Panda

Date:02.12.2024

Acknowledgments

Dear Reader,

"Relationships are the poetry of our lives, crafted through love, trust, and understanding."

This book exists because you— the curious, thinking, and searching for answers, are responsible for this book. Every word in these pages was inspired by your desire to understand the complexity of love and loyalty. I am grateful that you trusted me to lead you through this journey.

Thank you to the many voices, experiences, and stories that have shaped my work. These chapters have been enriched by each conversation and moment of vulnerability. Your encouragement and faith in me gave me strength and courage to continue.

This book is most important to you as a reader. It reflects your courage to learn, grow, and ask questions. I hope that it will help you to navigate through the complex web of relationships and provide clarity where needed.

You have opened your heart for this journey of love and connection.

Why Marriages Fail

We can find our struggles and desires for connection in the greatness of nature. Where rivers cut through the unyielding mountain ranges and ancient tree roots intertwine beneath the earth, there are reflections of ourselves. It is not because the river must flow, but rather because of an invisible pull towards the ocean. This pull mirrors our deepest yearning for love, intimacy, and understanding.

In our world of modernity, the glowing screens have replaced the warm glow from the hearth, and relationships are as fleeting as the leaves that the wind carries. There are many options available to us--faces on the apps that we swipe right and left, or conversations that reverberate like whispers through canyons. The abundance of choices hasn't brought us together but has instead spawned a disconnection epidemic. As cherry blossoms scatter in their prime before they reach full bloom, so too do many of today's relationships. They begin to grow but then wither due to unmet expectations or misaligned goals.

Infidelity is not always the result of physical desires, but rather from a deeper gap created by neglect, miscommunication, or a hurried lifestyle that does not allow for any connection. Indifference from a partner, lack of purpose, or unacknowledged life burdens can cause people to drift apart. Human relationships are prone to unpredictable, devastating storms. Yet, they also remind us that we have strength and fragility within.

A relationship, like the old oak branches that shelter countless animals, should be a haven of warmth, safety, and belonging. True intimacy is not just physical. It's in the understanding and acceptance of pain shared, in quiet support during times of uncertainty, and in unwavering presence throughout life's ups and downs. We can mirror Earth's strongest bonds by cultivating such a relationship. The sun embraces the earth unyieldingly, bringing life to the world even at night.

Marriage Vs Love

Marriage is easy, not love's tender fight,
Staying is easy, not valuing what's right.
Sharing a home is the simplest part,
But building a life takes a craftsman's heart.

Looking into someone's eyes can seem true,
Yet seeing their dreams is devotion's due.
Holding hands may feel warm at the start,
But holding their heart is the rarest art.

Starting a journey together feels light,
But navigating storms turns day into night.
Laughter is easy when life's skies are clear,
But crying together makes love sincere.

Touch may ignite, but does it sustain?
To make someone feel seen is love's domain.
Speaking comes quickly, like a fleeting breeze,
But listening with the heart is what frees.

So, cherish the layers, the fragile, the deep,
Love's not just promises you make, but ones you keep.

Infidelity or Reality

This poem is resonant because it touches the essence of who we are: not only do we seek a person to hold, but also a soul that understands us and a presence with nurturing qualities.

Life is short, and like a shooting star, it's fleeting. We must cherish the things that matter. The eternal is not transient or superficial. We find meaning in love. It is the root that grounds us and gives us wings.

Divergent Spouse

"Marriage is not merely a union of two souls, but a crucible where identities are forged, fractured, or freed."

Under the canopy of intertwined life bonds, vines sprout. Some bear fruit, while others are entwined tightly and smother the growth they purport to nourish. The ivy of a manipulative partner whispers support but creeps steadily to bind autonomy. They mimic spring rain but drown the roots below, leaving you gasping for the light and truth.

In the manipulator's embrace, love is reduced to a shadow, not a flame, flickering faintly in a gale of dominance. Love is a faint shadow in this gripping embrace. Even in this choking embrace, however, resilience stirs up like a wildflower between cracks seeking the sunlight. Every root seeks its freedom, every being its sky, for love is not bondage but boundless growth.

Every relationship unveils its essence—whether it nurtures, scars, or fades the spirit. To fathom these truths, one must first confront the profound influence of a manipulative companion.

Manipulators

Infidelity or Reality

A steady flame is often compared to affection in the complicated relationship landscape. It's warm, consistent, and nurturing. This is the force behind emotional stability, which allows people to grow without doubts. True affection comes from a steady presence, which comforts and nourishes the relationship.

What happens when the affection we feel becomes less comforting and more controlling?

When love is used to manipulate people, it becomes an instrument of control rather than a gift freely given.

Imagine feeling a rush of happiness and security as someone shows you affection. Warm, welcoming words and gestures make you feel valued. Imagine that warmth suddenly disappearing and leaving you feeling isolated. The *"inconsistent love"* tactic is based on this experience. Love is withheld to manipulate and create dependence.

Imagine riding a roller coaster where you experience highs that are exhilarating and satisfying, but they're short-lived, while lows last for ages, making you feel lost and confused. The manipulator uses inconsistent affection to create a similar feeling, where connection and joy are earned and not given. *One survivor describes a relationship in which they felt like the centre of the universe one moment and then left wondering what their place was the next.* The pattern was designed to keep their partners working constantly for approval and often changing their needs or desires to regain that short-lived, illusory feeling.

The strategy is based on the human need to feel connected and warm, which it corrupts. Love and affection are unpredictable, which becomes a way to control. You are hooked by the inconsistency as if you were chasing a high that is always out of reach.

The **push-pull dynamics** is a characteristic of manipulative love. The manipulator will show their partner love, gifts, and compliments one moment. The "push", or an intense show of passion or interest, is often used when the manipulator wants something back or needs to assert control. The attention is intoxicating and can create the illusion of intimacy. However, once they have gained power, the "pull" can make them cold, distant, or dismissive.

Manipulative love can limit growth and keep people in a cycle of unease. The emotional focus on getting affection leaves little time for personal development or reflection. It is the manipulator who creates doubt and makes people question their worth.

Start by realizing that true love is not an emotional game but a stable feeling. Individuals who recognize manipulative behaviours can create healthier relationships based on respect and mutual trust. Love should not make you feel like you are struggling for solid ground.

Manipulative Patterns

Gaslighting: Distorting Reality to Control Perception

Gaslighting is a sly method of psychological manipulation that alters the reality of things and diminishes perception. Gaslighting doesn't come out with loud declarations. Instead, it is concealed as a harmless rant or concern.

Reflecting on my experiences, I realise it wasn't a shocking revelation. It was more of a gradual unravelling -- a subtle, deliberate loss of faith in me.

It began slowly, as little whispers that grew into an erupting "torm. "Is that what ha? "My partner would inquire in a state of practised innocence. It was a simple question and almost funny in its casual way of speaking, but its implications were significant. Every time, I thought, was I sure? The experience that felt as vivid was now fragile and brittle, swaying like it was about to disappear when I pressed the subject too much.

Soon, doubt became my constant companion. The narrative shifted without warning. My memories of painful arguments or broken "promises--were changed "by his telling. "I never said that," he'd claim, "Your calm conviction made" me shiver. "You're imagining things again." The words of his conversation weaved the tapestry of his denial so complex that I was beginning to believe the structure. "Your sentence still echoes throughout my thoughts: "You're just too sensitive" With the one word, my feelings were manipulated against me. My pain became an issue, and my anger was a failure. He framed my feelings as overreactions, implying that my pain was not just invalid—it was evidence of my inadequacy. I learned to shrink, to filter my words and thoughts, terrified of confirming his accusations.

Gaslighting is like watching your reflection in a funhouse mirror—warped, unfamiliar, yet impossibly convincing. I started questioning every facet of myself: Was I overreacting? Was my memory so unreliable? Could I trust my mind? Slowly but surely, I began to disappear, swallowed by the persona my partner constructed for me—a volatile, untrustworthy version of myself that existed only in his story.

But it was more than my perception of reality they sought to control—it was my perception of worth. He snuffed me out of my faith and was replaced by a constant desire for his approval. I stopped making decisions that did not have my parents' approval, stopped trusting my instincts and stopped thinking that I would do it all by myself. I was bound to the version he had of me and struggled to breathe in a world that was filled with lies.

The breakthrough occurred in pieces. When I was in the middle of something, and he denied that I believed I'd done, a thought occurred: No, I'm not making up this. It was the feeling I had. It was only a whisper, and it was mine. Writing was the way to escape. I began recording every interaction, writing down my truth on a paper sheet before it was lost. My journal became my home base to remind me that my story was true even when people did not acknowledge it.

Rebuilding was arduous. Gaslighting doesn't just leave scars; it rewires you, making you question every instinct. But with time, I reclaimed what he had tried but didn't. I embraced my emotions as truths rather than inconveniences. I surrounded myself with people who didn't dismiss my pain but sat with it, offering compassion where I'd once found only dismissal.

Gaslighting is more than manipulation—it's an erasure of self. But healing taught me this: *my voice is mine, my memories are real, and my worth is unshakable*. No one else has the power to rewrite my reality.

Gaslighting patterns in relationships:

"That Never Happened"

When confronted about hurtful comments or actions, the gaslighter firmly denies the event ever occurred, even when evidence suggests otherwise.

Example:

You: "You said you'd pick me up at six and never showed."

Them: "I never said that. You must've dreamed it."

Twisting the Narrative

The gaslighter reframes events to make themselves appear as the victim and you as the aggressor.

Example:

You: "You hurt my feelings when you ignored me at dinner."

Them: "You're so dramatic. I ignored you because you wouldn't stop embarrassing me."

Undermining Your Memory

They subtly plant doubt about your ability to remember things accurately.

Example:

Them: "You're so forgetful lately. Are you sure you're okay? You can't even keep simple things straight."

Disguised as Concern

They use fake concern to make you question your stability.

Example:

Them: "I'm worried about you. You seem really off lately. Maybe you should talk to someone about it."

Minimizing Your Feelings

Your emotions are trivialized, making you feel unreasonable for expressing them.

Example:

You: "I feel upset when you criticize me in front of others."

Them: "Wow, you're really blowing this out of proportion."

Projecting Their Behavior Onto You

The gaslighter accuses you of doing the very things they are guilty of.

Example:

Them: "You're the one who's always lying and manipulating me. I can't trust you anymore."

Withholding Information

They intentionally leave out details and then blame you for not knowing them.

Example:

You: "Why didn't you tell me about the change in plans?"

Them: "I told you—you just weren't paying attention as usual."

Eroding Your Support System

They isolate you by convincing you that others are untrustworthy.

Example:

Them: "Your friends don't really care about you—they're just using you. I'm the only one who's honest with you."

Reinforcing Negative Traits

They repeatedly label you with negative characteristics to erode your self-worth.

Example:

Them: "You're so overly emotional. No wonder people find it hard to take you seriously."

Shifting Blame

They deflect accountability by making everything your fault, even when they are clearly at fault.

Example:

You: "Why did you cancel our plans without telling me?"

Them: "I wouldn't have had to cancel if you weren't always so demanding. This is on you.

Cutting Off Support Systems

His gaze captured my attention when I saw my partner for the first time. The intensity and depth of the gaze were so intense that it would make an excellent subject for a novel. His words, wrapped up in love, would say, *"Nobody understands you as I do"*. At first, I thought he was right. I liked seeing someone look at me and spend so much time on me. Over time, though, it became clear that his affection for me was more concerned with control than power.

The first thing that happened was not a dramatic ultimatum or an apparent demand. It came as whispers, placed carefully to undermine my relationship with those I love. His voice was gentle but full of implication as he asked, *"Are they there for you?"* He made me question my friends, and I began to doubt them. He planted seeds that grew slowly until I started to turn down family events and invitations because of my belief that they did not understand me as he understood.

His tone was soft and almost depressed. He said, "But I listen." His tone was soft and almost sad. When I separated myself from a person, I experienced a peculiar loyalty. Cutting off ties showed my loyalty to people who always supported me.

It's not something that happens suddenly; isolation is woven throughout our lives. As time passed, I began to notice how much my life had centred around him. My decisions, which I used to make confidently before, were now subjected to his judgment. When I spoke about my career goals, he suggested that the job could be too demanding. What if you change? The implied message was that anything I did to escape him would waste time.

Without the voices of my friends and family, I lost sight of myself. My self-worth decreased without the voices of family and friends. As if my dreams belonged to somebody else, they seemed far away. Although I said I was content, I still missed being the independent, vibrant person I once was.

A friend of mine reached out to me. She said, "I'm missing you." "Are you OK?" Her words moved me. Then, I realized how much had been sacrificed and how much I had buried to be accepted into his world. But breaking free felt impossible. Without him, who would I be? Was it possible to re-establish the relationships I abandoned?

At first, it was slow--hesitant text messages to old friends and awkward calls to the family. The responses I received surprised me. They said, "We are here," with kindness and compassion. A friend told me, "You do not owe anyone your happiness. Your love made me remember something I'd forgotten: I am capable, strong and worthy.

It took a lot of work to leave. It wasn't easy to regain confidence in oneself. When I returned to the people who loved me, fragments of my old self began to return. True love doesn't create barriers; it lifts your spirits. Then, I made a promise never to let anyone down again.

The moment that you take back your voice, you are taking back your life. This is what I have learned. "I'm still recovering, but I am surrounded by love that I thought I lost and, more importantly, love that I forgot to give myself.

Gaslighting patterns in relationships:

Questioning the Loyalty of Loved Ones

Manipulator: "Do you think your friend has your back? She always talks about herself and doesn't ask about you."

Partner: "I don't know… maybe she's just busy?"

Manipulator: "Busy or selfish? I hate seeing you give your energy to people who don't value you as I do."

Subtle Criticism of Friends

Manipulator: "Your friend is always so negative. It must be exhausting for you to deal with that all the time."

Partner: "I guess she can be a little pessimistic…"

Manipulator: "Exactly. I don't want you to get dragged down by her bad energy."

Claiming Special Understanding

Manipulator: "Your family doesn't get you, do they? I see how unique you are, but they seem stuck in their old ways."

Partner: "They've always been a little traditional, I guess."

Manipulator: "It's OK. I'll always see the real you, even if they don't."

Encouraging Distance from Loved Ones

Manipulator: "Do you want to spend your Saturday at your cousin's party? I was hoping we could have a quiet night together."

Partner: "I don't know, I kind of promised I'd go…"

Manipulator: "You've been so stressed lately. You deserve to rest. They'll understand."

Implying Loved Ones Don't Care

Manipulator: "Have you noticed how your brother never asks about me? It's like he doesn't even care that we're together."

Partner: "I'm sure he's just busy."

Manipulator: "Busy, or he just doesn't respect our relationship?"

Discrediting Advice from Others

Manipulator: "What did your friend say about our argument? That we should break up? She's always been jealous of what we have."

Partner: "No, she just said I should think about what makes me happy."

Manipulator: "Exactly. She doesn't want you to be happy with me because she doesn't have anyone in her life."

Framing Loved Ones as Interfering

Manipulator: "Why does your mom always need to know what's going on in our relationship? It's like she doesn't trust you to make your own choices."

Partner: "She just worries about me sometimes."

Manipulator: "You're not a child. She needs to let you live your life."

Making Loved Ones the "Enemy"

Manipulator: "Your friend told you I'm controlling? Wow, I guess she doesn't want to see you happy."

Partner: "I don't think she meant it that way."

Manipulator: "Of course she did. She's just trying to come between us."

Guilt-Tripping Over Prioritizing Others

Manipulator: "You're going out with your friends again? I thought tonight was our night."

Partner: "We didn't really have plans…"

Manipulator: "I just miss you when you're gone. But I guess they're more important."

Discouraging Dreams to Avoid Independence

Manipulator: "That new job sounds great, but won't it take up all your time? I'd miss you so much if you're always busy with work."

Partner: "It would mean longer hours, but it's a great opportunity."

Manipulator: "I don't know… I feel like we'd drift apart. Is it really worth that risk?"

Shifting Blame and Eliciting Sympathy

It began as a dream like manipulative relationships typically tend to. Each word of his was the warmth of a hug, wrapping me in love and affection. Yet, at some point, I lost my bearings. Love slowly turned into a maze of guilt, and victimhood was his weapon as I was the shadow of my former self.

The cracks were tiny, barely noticeable. When I expressed a concern, he would sigh and reply, *"I only acted that way because I thought you didn't care."* This sounded sensible and almost soft until the pattern was obvious. Each conversation turned back towards him, his emotions or his sorrow. It started as love, but it turned out to be an intricate manipulation, like an improvised show in which I was a puppet continually trying to correct the harm he said I did.

"You're so sensitive," the man would say every time I would try to convey the hurt he caused by his words. It made me question myself: Was I too sensitive? Too demanding? His story of being manipulated and hurt by the world was crafted in such a beautiful way that I regularly was sceptical about the truth of my own life. Every argument would end the same way. He recounted his battles in a way that made him appear as the victim of an unforgiving universe. *"I didn't mean it that way; it's just how I was raised,"* the man would say while I was with a sense of guilt at bringing this up.

In the evening, I was able to describe my feelings about his actions. I was hoping for some understanding or perhaps a bit of remorse. But instead, he wept--deep stomach-churning sobs, telling me how he was unloved and how each mistake that he committed was a result of the scars that he'd suffered. *"If only you understood how hard it is for me,"* the man spoke, and then, it was that I was person apologizing, helping his hand, and comforting those who had hurt me.

The psychological burden was omnipresent. Slowly, I lost touch with my emotions. He assured me that my fears were overblown and my anxieties were unfounded. I gave up on myself and instead put all my energy into making him whole again. But, regardless of the amount of love I gave to him, it wasn't enough. The only way he came out was to shrug off blame, continue to be an innocent victim and trap me in his web of lies and shame.

The moment of truth came after a conversation with a friend that was a constant reminder of the way I felt: *"Love shouldn't feel like a guessing game."* I realized the constantly ambiguous state of affairs and the continuous attempts to figure out his motives weren't normal. It's not supposed to make you doubt the value of your life. After a while, I started to realize the ruse was a purposeful effort to evade accountability and to keep me tied.

Moving on took work. In the past, I believed that I could repair everything by working harder and becoming a better lover. Then, I discovered that love is not able to thrive in a world where manipulation is the main ingredient. As Brene Brown put it, *"Daring to set boundaries is about having the courage to love ourselves, even when we risk disappointing others."* Letting go was a courageous act as a way to claim the stories he attempted to manage.

In the present, being compassionate shouldn't be a reason to let toxicity go without being noticed. Empathy for another person's discomfort doesn't have to mean you'll give up your tranquillity. True love doesn't play the role of a victim. It promotes development in accountability, respect, and passion for one another. My conviction is that I'll not settle for anything less than the best.

Withholding Affection as a Tool for Control

It is a symphony of love; it is a profound exchange where two souls come together in harmony. When love is conditioned and conditioned, it transforms into a calculating weapon. It was a lesson I witnessed firsthand through the course of a relationship, which left me doubting my value and my understanding of love.

The onset was subtle, as the shadow of a dark shadow slipped into the areas of my life. I became distant every time I took a step that the person disagreed with or did not manage to meet his requirements. I remember one evening vividly. I'd opted not to cancel the arrangement with my spouse, after which came one week of no texts or calls but a space. This wasn't a fight; it was punishment.

He also used his physical proximity as leverage. "I don't feel close to you right now," He would tell me, avoiding the possibility of a hug or even a kiss until I expressed my apology for something I was unable to explain. When the days turned into months, his support turned into a currency that I struggled hard to win.

"Love isn't supposed to feel like a debt you're endlessly trying to repay. "

With the pressure of unconditional love, my self-worth started to diminish. Every glance or smirk was an insult. Am I not worth the attention? Am I not worthy of being noticed? My once-inspiring ambitions faded because I put all my energy into pleasing a particular person. I was afraid of the uncertainty that might cause him to leave.

The most devastating moment occurred when I looked into the mirror and could not even recognize myself. It was hard to see the confident and joyful person that I was before. In reality, I was an unreliable shadow who was constantly looking for approval from someone who handed the praise sparingly, much like food to a hungry bird.

"The love you fight for should lift you higher, not weigh you down with doubt and insecurity. "

Being aware that I was a part of the cycle of toxic love was a sign. Recognizing that I was in a love-based relationship was the first step to the freedom I was seeking.

1. **Trust Your Instincts**

One night, I lay awake replaying the countless moments of tension and withholding. My gut screamed what my heart didn't want to acknowledge—this wasn't love. It was control.

2. **Set Boundaries**

I learned to voice my feelings, even risking another silent treatment. "I won't accept this kind of treatment," I would say, and for the first time, I stood firm.

3. **Pursue External Perspectives**

Talking to my parents was my lifeline. They reminded me that love should be a sanctuary, not a battlefield.

4. **Cultivate Self-Worth**

As time passed, I slowly began to restore myself. I rediscovered painting as a hobby of my past and was able to relive the joy of expressing myself fully without requiring anyone's approval but just my satisfaction.

It was as if you were getting out of the dark storm and into the sun. As I've discovered, love is unchanging and doesn't change due to disagreements or mistakes. It's not a contract; It's a relationship.

If you're feeling stuck by the spectre of love that is conditional, I'm offering this advice: *You deserve love that isn't accompanied by an agenda. A true love won't leave you wondering about your value.*

Masking Insecurity with Control

Initially, I believed that jealousy was a sign of Love, an intense desire to show someone cared for their loved ones. The reality, however, was a different story. The conversation began with basic questions like "Where were you? " Or "Who were you talking to?" Initially, it was like a hug or even a sense of security because I felt like I was significant enough to someone else to value me that much. Then, these questions became more sharp and more frequent in terms of curiosity but more focused on control. That which I had thought of as affection became a feeling of suffocation.

My relationship was tainted by jealousy as a shadow. It was inconspicuous and barely noticeable initially. The initial reaction was innocent--a quip here, joke here. However, over time, the conversation grew into constant suspense and baseless allegations. "Why didn't you tell me about your plans earlier?" "Are you hiding something? " These questions cut more than I ever imagined. I felt as if I was constantly on trial in an effort to prove my loyalty to a person who seemed to be eager to come up with motives to question me.

Monitoring constantly robbed me of my peace. The issue wasn't only about where I was; it was all about the slightest particular-- who texted me, why I smiled at someone or even the clothes I put on. The temptation to be jealous became a jail that was built from the fear of being judged and insecurity.

Possessiveness disguises itself as Love with the disguise of concern. *"I'm just looking out for you,"* the man would say with an expression that felt like an iron chain that was tightening around me. The decisions I made about my life, my relationships, and my choices did not belong to me anymore. It started innocently, with a suggestion on how to dress or an informal comment on a friend. However, it quickly became controlling my schedule, deciding my acquaintances and managing every step.

A few days ago, I cancelled the long-anticipated vacation because "it would make him uncomfortable." I thought it was an act of compromise; however, in my heart, I knew that it was a sign of surrender. My perspective slowed when he grew as the leash of his control got tighter for every concession I made.

For a long time, I believed in his words. "I only do this because I love you," his soft and almost prayerful voice. The feeling of Love was like a huge load rather than a cosy hug. The confusion was the most challenging part. Was it really because they were looking for me? Was I engulfed in his desire to be in command?

It's awe-inspiring how quickly love could turn into manipulative. Sincere Love is empowering, but this twisting version of it has made me question my wits or my worthiness and even my self-reliance. *"You don't need them; you have me,"* he would insist until he was total.

In retrospect, the impact on my self-esteem was huge. I began to doubt my own decisions as I began to doubt even the most minor decisions. Friends dwindled. My career stagnated, and I became the person I had been--a bright, confident person--was changed by someone uncertain and scared.

Then I realized I wasn't losing time; I was losing myself. My desire to avoid conflicts kept me in a rut. However, the price was far too much. "If I'm not me anymore," I thought to myself "what's left for me to love? "

The moment I broke free was not a dramatic event; it was more of the result of a few small, peaceful, rebellious moments. It began by relying on my gut instincts. If anything felt off, then it was probably wrong. It was scary to set boundaries, yet it was liberating. "No, I won't share my location all the time. " "Yes, I'm planning to go out with my buddies. " Every line I drew was a brick on the wall I had built to defend myself.

The importance of talking to other people was paramount. The voices of my friends and family reaffirmed my past before shadows started to appear. Their constant help was just my light to get my eyes back.

In the end, I learned for myself. I learned about manipulation and heard stories of other people who had been through similar circumstances, and slowly, I cranked up the determination to go on my own. The words of one victim were awe-inspiring: *"Love is freedom, not fear. "*

It is now clear that Love isn't an abyss; it is a nurturing force. The love of a person doesn't want control; it is completely trusting. Besiege and jealousy do not protect relationships; they ruin relationships. It was the most complex and most influential act of self-love that I've performed.

For anyone who is on this road, trust yourself. It is your right to have a relationship that lifts your self-esteem instead of tearing you to pieces. Your worth is in every moment of your journey towards freedom.

Using Guilt and Fear to Manipulate

I was once at the end of an emotional pit and was engulfed by the dark influence of the tangled web. Every move I made was filled with guilt and fear and an invisible puller pushing me back each time I attempted to claim my freedom. The words, "After all I've done for you, how could you?" were a constant refrain in my head and was a continual reminder that gnawed away at my confidence in myself. Then, in the process of peeling away the layers of my confusion, I realized it was not love; it was a form of emotional blackmail.

It started slowly, inconspicuously, like an undercurrent at the ocean. Small gestures became significant sacrifices. "Remember that time I was up late to assist you? What could I do to make you feel less today??" However, as time went on, it became apparent that these gestures were not a sign of affection; they were devices to control. His guilt was insufferable.

It was also a factor in fear and cast long shadows over the conversations. "If you quit and I'm not able to come back," I was caught by the burden of guilt that he placed on me and the constant worry of being blamed for the root of his pain.

As time passed, I began to doubt my judgement. I was no longer able to trust myself to make choices. Every decision was fraught with the possibility of emotional repercussions. My self-confidence waned, followed by the constant worry about not doing enough or not giving enough. The intelligent, curious and vibrant individual I was once persona too focused on settling the demands of others to pursue my ambitions.

The realization occurred when I was having a chat with a person who inquired, "Do you ever feel loved or just obligated?" This inquiry stayed with me for a while and helped me unravel the web of manipulative behaviour that was entangling me. I noticed patterns, such as how the disagreements would always end with my feeling guilty, and the "love" seemed contingent on my being a good citizen.

Retrospectiving my own emotions was an awakening. Instead of feeling secure, I experienced anxiety. Instead of happiness, it was fear. This realization was painful. However, they were essential.

It was a challenging task to break free. It felt like walking on burning wood, but every step brought me back to my freedom. I began by setting boundaries in my life and then making sure not to say no without giving reasons. "I need to prioritize myself," I stated to him at one point, my voice shaking but determined. The backlash was immediate--accusations of selfishness, tears meant to guilt me back into submission--but I held firm.

The process of educating myself about manipulation tactics made me stronger. I read, thought, and sought out the opinions of my trusted family and friends. He showed me that love isn't a chain around the person. It binds but instead frees them. Slowly, I swapped fear for the courage to take on responsibilities and respect for myself.

As time passed, I reconstructed myself one piece at a time. I learned to respect my desires and trust my gut instincts. The emotional blackmail was at first the labyrinth of no escape; however, by establishing boundaries and looking for the truth, I was able to find the escape.

Today, I am sharing my experience with those who are trapped by it. Remember that the value you have does not depend on other people's needs. The actual connection isn't based on the fear of guilt or shame but instead through mutual respect and affection. Find your strength by taking one step at a time. It is essential to have relationships that nourish your soul, not smother the strength of it.

Disregarding Personal Limits

There was a point that I lived through where the boundaries that separated "mine" and "his" began to blur. The beginning was small, an object borrowed with no request and decisions taken "for my good," or even a joke on my part that I laugh at. "He doesn't mean harm," I'd say to myself, squirting away the numbness that came over my brain.

However, boundaries don't just have to be regarding possessions or options but about respect. This disrespect didn't cease. My objections were slowly ignored. A "no" became negotiable, my privacy a wide-open door. The man would scroll through my phone and justify it by saying, "What are you hiding?" I did not have anything to hide, but I was exposed. It felt like my thoughts were being spoken to without my consent.

It was hard to tell initially. His actions were concealed under the guise of concern and care. "I'm doing this for you," He would declare I believed him since I believed it. Yet, believing doesn't remove the pain that is felt the moment someone begins to view yourself through the lens of.

A few nights ago, I was being silent after an argument. His determination destroyed my boundaries. My voice in my head, just whispering, then said, "This isn't right." This was the first time that I was genuinely listening to the voice that was in me.

The overstepping of a boundary doesn't show itself immediately. It is gradually introduced incrementally until you finally get up to realise that you've lost parts of yourself. The stifling effect of it impeded my growth and made me feel like I was reluctant to make choices, afraid of his approval. My confidence was dwindling because I was constantly unsure if my thoughts were confirmed. I began to look like an image of the person I used to be.

It was then the most challenging step: coming back to me. The first step was to say "no" and mean it. If he didn't, then I repeated it with a firm stance. It was not easy. My hands were shaking, and my voice shook, but I stood firm. "Boundaries aren't walls," I said to him a few days ago. "His door with lock, and I hold the key."

I began to study the way he behaved and his statements. I observed the pattern: his apology, then he'd keep doing the same thing. *"Consistency is integrity,"* I thought to myself to believe the evidence I saw instead of what was said to me.

The ability to see things from a different perspective was transformational. My mentors and friends assisted me in recognizing what I didn't see say: this wasn't love; it was a matter of control. Love is respectful and doesn't violate.

The process of leaving wasn't about just moving away; it was about walking toward me. I was surrounded by people who were supportive of my choices rather than trying to challenge them. I found myself reconnected to my beliefs along with my dreams, passions, and voice.

"Your worth isn't negotiable," I frequently remind myself of this. The boundaries aren't obstacles to love. It can be bridges that allow the truth and respect. In that regard, I was able to find freedom, the freedom to develop, believe again, and fully be myself.

When Love is a Lie

I once believed I had found the kind of love that novels romanticize--intense, all-consuming, and unshakable. However, over time, what I thought was love started to feel like sand, taking me deeper into a void I was unable to leave. The first sign of affection was too ideal as if I were the centre of the universe. "You're all I need," I'd hear him declare, his eyes locking on mine with a tense passion. In the beginning, I was convinced that it was because of love. But now I realise that it was really control that was disguised as love.

The effect was stunning. Flowers on my desk after I'd had a bad day, snorted promises of a better future together, and all mixed with icy silences whenever they didn't live up to their requirements. The moments of withdrawal caused me to ponder my own. Was I ungrateful? Impossible? I attempted harder to please them like an anxious person trying to find lost ground. "I love you when you're like this," the man once told me, an expression that was so sweet but also so intelligent that it cut into the heart of my self-confidence.

There was a subtle gaslighting that followed in the beginning. "I never said that; you must be imagining things." The repetition of a statement enough times could cause you to lose your perception of real-world reality. I began to doubt my memory, re-evaluating my every step. Was I too sensitive? Overly demanding? My self-confidence was diminishing like the sand washed away by a constant flood. My apologizing ended each argument. I was often uncertain of the things I'd made a mistake but determined to bring harmony.

The loneliness began to creep in slowly. "Why do you even need them when you have me?" Friends turned into distant numbers that were reduced to numbers on my cell phone that I rarely called. My world shrank down to the level of my husband's acceptance. While I was not aware, I became utterly dependent on their moods and their whims.

One of the most brutal tactics was conditional love. It was a conditional love: obedience to a certain degree, compliance, and silence. *"If you truly loved me, you'd understand."* The love was not real but an exchange, one in which I paid more than what I got. Yet, I continued in the belief that if I did my best and worked harder, I'd earn that love I thought I could have.

However, one day, the fog went away. It was a calm period, a day with clarity. I remembered the person I was prior to me. I recalled my laugh; I remembered my dreams, my laughter, and my voice. Then I realized I needed to recover them.

It began to heal slowly. I started trusting my gut and recognizing that the discomfort I sensed was the soul's way of warning me. I was able to contact old acquaintances and apologise for my absence, relying on their constant commitment. I learned how to define boundaries. Not walls but guidelines that represent my values. "No, I won't tolerate that."

The most important thing I learned was that love isn't an award to be won or a chain that needs to be worn. Love is an opportunity to be a refuge and not a trap. It's free and not tied to a person's demands.

If you're trapped in a similar web of confusion, be aware that You deserve better. Find your voice and move towards the light of actual, unwavering love. It will be there, beginning by giving love to yourself.

Identifying Patterns Over Time

I've had the experience of being lost in a romantic relationship that felt like a walk-through sand, each step leading me further into the fog. It was at first to be perfect. *"This is it,"* I thought to myself, being swept away by brief moments of passionate love. However, soon, the love was replaced with cold, distant and sarcastic comments. My insanity gnawed at me. I started looking for validation, but I could not get it.

The cycle continued for a long time. There were times of happiness and joy, which were followed by nights of worry and fear. *"Am I overreacting?* "I'd think while he dismissed my concerns by uttering gaslighting comments like *"You're imagining things"* In time, I began to lose my sense of reality, and loneliness grew while I got further away, far from the ones who nurtured me.

The other day, I stumble onto a notebook I'd put aside for a while. When I turned the pages, patterns began to appear. Each page showed the same cycle of love and disapproval. *"How did I not see this before?"* I asked. It was clear. Time revealed what my soul was unwilling to believe, and that was that I was caught in a web of manipulation.

Recognizing this, I began modestly but with firmness. I imposed boundaries, telling myself, "This behaviour is not okay." I looked up books, articles or anything else to learn about how people were using tactics against me as I surrounded myself with people whom I'd left behind and re-building the support network.

In retrospect, it was the process of finding the patterns I was able to recognise that helped me. Recording my thoughts and reflections over time gave me an understanding. That clarity brought me confidence and the determination to tell myself, "I deserve better."

If you're stuck by the same cycle, keep in mind that patterns can't necessarily mean anything. Look around, consider and then take action. Your worth is more significant than what you can achieve within the limits of manipulation.

Neglect Relationship

Understanding the Dynamics of Neglect in Relationships

Relations are fragile and delicate and need nurturing in order to flourish. I can remember experiencing an invisible wall created between us. It was a silence that wasn't only quiet but isolated. *"Neglect is the absence of something essential, "*I was thinking, and the lack of something was gradually persuading us to break up.

The silence began with tiny issues. I'd tell my story--a brief story or displeasure--only for it to be met with an uninvolved nod or a partial "That's nice." He was not interested; in fact, I believed that he did. The lack of communication made me feel unimportant. I've said, *"It feels like I'm screaming into a void,"* but this was not noticed. Neglecting your emotions is like gradual erosion. It doesn't cause a break-up in an instant but slowly removes the base.

There were also the unremembered occasions:

- Family dinners that weren't attended

- Unremembered dates

- A lack of time for chores

I felt like I was the sole bearer of this burden and physically active in our everyday life; however, I was alone in every sense. I recall standing on the counter, enveloped with dishes unwashed and wondering, *"Is this partnership or a solitary journey? "* The absence of physical activity wasn't an issue of absence but rather an absence of a shared effort and the imbalance which made me tired and longing to be supported.

The most significant disconnect resulted from my inability to accept what was essential to me: my beliefs and values. If I mentioned my religious practices, people dismissed it, telling me, "That's not my thing." In time, I felt as if a piece of me was discarded. I was beginning to question whether there was a place for me as a whole in this situation or if it was necessary to separate myself in order to maintain the peace.

The healing process began after I realized that the underlying causes of neglect aren't always intentional. It's often unintentional, caused by miscommunication or distraction. However, the hurt it creates is accurate, and dealing with it takes effort from both parties.

- I was able to speak up without feeling resentful. In one instance, I stated, "I need you to listen, not just hear me." A small change in my perception led us to a better understanding.

- We began by sharing our responsibilities. Making meals together, even things that were as basic as washing the dishes, were acts of collaboration instead of a series of chores that were purely individual.

- We discovered ways of honouring our spiritual beliefs. The lighting of a candle or taking time to be quiet to reflect helped us bridge our spiritual divide.

Neglect flourishes in silence; however, healing starts with acknowledgement. If we let go of those cracks in our relationship and instead confronted them, we saw that love could be strengthened than previously. Remember, *"Love isn't just about presence; it's about showing up every day for the little things, even when it's hard."*

The Subtle Signs of Emotional Withdrawal

It took a long time to unravel, which was barely noticeable initially, like an invisible thread that was pulled until the whole fabric of the connection started to unravel. I recall how we would talk to each other with ease, conversations that flowed effortlessly in laughter, accompanied by shared hopes. Then, the conversations became more sporadic, and the silences became more frequent. I'd ask him what his experience of the day was when I asked him, and his answer would be a short, slack response. "It was fine," he'd reply, eyes focusing elsewhere. But I was still stumbling with the burden of those unspoken words that served to hold us together.

There were days that his touch was absent as if the touch was an obligation, not a gesture of affection. It wasn't only about physical intimacy but also about gazing into one another's eyes and being able to feel seen. I started to worry about those moments when he'd slide away, not physically but rather with his heart. I'd try to reach out, but I cannot validate. However, I'd reach out for connections but be met with a slew of explanations, disinterested glances or a cold reluctance that was more painful than any words could ever be.

I'm not sure when this occurred, but his awareness of my difficulties was apparent to disappear. I've once confided to him concerning my concerns, hoping for an embrace that would be comforting and reassuring compassion. His response instead was indifferent and dismissive. *"You're overthinking it,"* the man declared. At that point, I was more isolated, as if I'd been able to keep it a secret. His indifference was the shadow of a person, obscuring the most shining parts of us.

The days he sat by himself, I was increased in length, surrounded by the glimmer of a screen or pages from an old book. I was awed by the moments of quiet in the same space, regardless of whether we were engaged in different activities. However, this time was different. It was a gap and not an enthralling silence. It was like an obstacle I was unable to reach, and I was stuck on the other side in a state of confusion, wondering if I had become the only person in his life.

The excitement we used to feel during movies, walks, and spontaneous adventures was changed by a deep lacklusterness. "You go ahead," the man would say every time, every time; each rejection felt like a new nail to our coffins of mutual satisfaction. My plans started to seem like desperate efforts to revive an old flame that he was never interested in tending.

His love waned at first but in the form of a gradual, painful loss. The kisses turned into regular, and the hug was a joke. "I love you" felt as though he was saying it from habit, not directly from his heart. But I was glued to the words and hoped he was true despite everything suggesting that he was not.

The process of recognizing emotions was the first step towards greater clarity. The focus wasn't on blaming others; instead, it was about identifying the cracks and making the decision to either repair them or accept that they would happen. I began opening conversations with a gentle touch by employing "I feel" rather than "he did" to avoid being defensive. "I feel distant from you," I said to him in one night, my voice twitching. For the first time in months, I didn't even look at him.

We sought assistance together. The counselling process became a place where we were able to confront the gap that was growing between us. We learned how to listen, the power of vulnerability, and the value of little conscious acts of kindness.

Then, slowly, we began to tie the knots in. It wasn't perfect, but not easy; however, we did it with the belief that love isn't simply a sentiment but the choice we make daily to bridge the distance.

Understanding the Root Causes

I stood once at the crossroads of my life, looking into the void between us. No silence was spoken; it was the work that silence kept from me. I was sure we were in love with each other, but during our relationship, the bond dissolved into an intricate web of miscommunication and feelings of distance. There wasn't one single thing that brought us to this point; it was the result of unsaid things that were subtle and unspoken--a structure I had to break to salvage what we'd created.

"Why can't we just talk? " I have once mused to myself during an argument that ended with doors shut, not hearts opened. The process of emotional detachment didn't happen overnight. It developed like an ivy that swarmed through cracks and became invasive. It was due to a variety of factors, including past traumas, social expectations, and the influence of good-hearted families and friends.

These fights were not battles; it was a retreat. We were both lacking the ability to manage disputes. When the conflict was brewing, and he was unable to resolve it, he shut down while I was able to over-analyze each phrase. It was like we were all locked up in an area, and we were scared to step into it. *"I don't want to fight,"* He would declare, but his real intention was: *"I don't know how to fight without losing you."*

I realized that we're both victims of our fears and inability to face anxiety, resulting in a gap between us. I read about conflict resolution and came to the notion that fighting isn't just about winning but about being able to understand. As time passed, I was able to conduct our conversations by focusing on the problem instead of blaming and opening doors instead of constructing walls.

The emotional withdrawal he experienced wasn't just all about me. It was all about his own. He would often talk about the feeling of "not good enough," but he would never express that explicitly. This was evident in his reluctance to show vulnerability because letting me into his life might expose his shortcomings. It was difficult for me to understand initially, and I mistakenly believed the distance was ignorance.

In the evening, he confessed, *"Sometimes, I feel like you'd be better off without me."* The words that they spoke of broke a part within me. Not in a way that caused me to leave; however, it caused me to want to remain and assist him in seeing the person I saw myself. I began to praise his character in small ways by making him aware of his importance--not just for his accomplishments and not for what is.

The shadows of his early years were a constant presence in our friendship. The parents did not talk about emotional issues; they just put them aside, and he grew to believe that vulnerability is a sign of a weak point. "My mom never said 'I love you,'" the man admitted in one instance, with an uneasy smile in his mouth.

I realized that he didn't hide his love; he didn't know what to say about the emotion. We began peeling away all the layers from his life in search of the remnants of unresolved injuries. Therapy was our friend as a safe space in which he could confront his past with no fear of being judged.

Beyond our personal stories and experiences, other forces were at work. Families, friends and expectations of culture weaved an unsettling story that was difficult to avoid.

Family members valued appearances above feelings. *"Don't air your dirty laundry,"* his mother used to say often to discourage open dialogue. This was his ethos, believing that opening up about issues was equal to failing.

If I had suggested that couples counsel, He hesitated. *"What will my family think?"* "What will my family think?" he demanded. It took months of gentle persuasion for him to realize that asking for help was not a weakness; it was a strength.

Our close friends also affected our relationship in subtle ways. Friends would dismiss emotional issues with phrases such as, *"She's overthinking again,"* which exacerbated their tendency to withdraw. My companions, while friendly, sometimes fuelled my anger by encouraging me to ask for more instead of seeking to understand.

I learned the value of filtering out advice. Then, we began to surround ourselves with those who were more supportive of growth than separation, forming an influence circle that helped rather than affected our bonds.

Tradition's weight weighed heavy on us. Growing up in a society that valued stoicism among men as well as emotional work for women, we consciously slipped into roles that hindered our bonds. He was compelled to be the one who provided, and I was tasked to take care of the children. *"I thought if I provided for you, that would be enough,"* He once said. But it wasn't, not due to the fact that he failed. We both needed more than what society moulds could provide.

The fact that he lived close to his parents was a further source of stress. Their values often conflicted with ours, causing tension that we never could resolve. *"They're my family,"* He would say defensively when I expressed my displeasure. It took him some time to realize that prioritizing our relationships wasn't about abandoning his family; it was about establishing boundaries that honoured us each.

Navigating Towards Change

It takes work to navigate the complexity of today's relationships, especially in a world that is fast-paced and full of expectations. Growth and healing are only possible when you address the issues that lie beneath, both internal and external. Every relationship has its own unique set of challenges. But the steps to understanding, reconciliation, and flourishing remain universal.

Recognition and Awareness

The foundation for healing is acknowledgment. You can think of it as naming ghosts to make him lose his ability to haunt. One friend told me how his partner shut down when he disagreed and retreated into silence. He took it personally for years and believed that this was an act of rejection. He realized through conversations that it was an old defense mechanism from his partner's childhood, where speaking out often resulted in punishment.

He began to see this, and the blame started to fade. Curiosity took over. Instead of saying, "You ignore me every time," he began to ask, "What is going on in your mind when we disagree?" This awareness replaced the frustration and created a place for compassion. Brene Brown once stated, *"Vulnerability leads to connection and a sense of worthiness." "*

Developing Conflict Resolution Skills

Conflict can be an excellent opportunity to grow. Communication is the key. My partner used the "I Feel" method instead of accusatory statements like "You Never" He tried saying, "You don't listen to me" instead of "You are never listening."

It's like opening the window of a stuffy, stuffy room to let in fresh air. At first, it's difficult because defensiveness is ingrained in our minds. Over time, however, the small language changes helped to build a stronger foundation of mutual understanding.

Building Self-Worth

In relationships, self-esteem plays an essential but often silent role. One of my close friends spent many years trying to hide his achievements from his partner because he believed that his work was not worthy of recognition. The partner had to be persistent and encouraging, saying things like "I'm so proud of you for this project" or "I appreciate how dedicated you are."

The same principle applies to relationships in the modern world. Both partners must be reminded of the value of each other outside of the relationship, not only of his love. Relationships flourish when one partner gains confidence.

Healing from Trauma

It's a big job, but necessary to liberate yourself. One person that I knew carried betrayal scars into all of his relationships. The therapy saved him, not because it erased his memories but because it allowed him to rewrite the narrative.

It was no longer "I'm hurt because I'm not good enough," but *"I'm hurt because another person couldn't deal with his flaws."* The weight was lifted off of his shoulders, and he could now approach love again. Healing doesn't necessarily mean forgetting but reclaiming the story.

Challenging Cultural Norms

Cultural narratives are often suffocating. As a child, I was told that the love test is endurance. Another friend said that she believed in the same thing and stayed in a relationship that was emotionally draining because "that is what love means--sticking with it."

Love is not about sacrifices that never end; love is about growth for both parties. The couple challenged the narrative by stepping outside of their comfort zones and accepting that setting boundaries is an act of love. Esther Perel said: *"The quality and depth of your relationships will determine the quality of life."*

Building a Supportive Network

Supportive communities are transformative. It's like planting a fertile garden by surrounding yourself with those who are authentic. A couple that I respect started hosting dinners with friends who had similar values. He shared his hopes, struggles, and joys.

The gatherings were safe spaces, reminding the participants that they didn't have to conform to societal norms. The journey was to be navigated together without judgment.

Modern relationships thrive on intentionality, mutual respect, and a willingness to learn from one another. By embracing vulnerability, communicating openly, challenging outdated norms, and surrounding ourselves with support, we create bonds that withstand the storms of life.

In the words of Rumi, *"Your job is not to search for love but to simply seek out and identify all the barriers that have been built within you against it."*

While we worked through the layers, we experienced something wonderful. We found ourselves once more. He began to speak his emotions while I discovered how to accept them and not judge them. Then we started to celebrate small wins--a touching conversation, a dispute that was resolved through mutual understanding, and a time of sharing vulnerability.

"I feel closer to you than I ever have," he spoke one night. His voice was soft yet certain. These words are a testimony to the extent we've come, not solely as individuals, but as a team willing to take on something worthy of saving.

It has been my experience that love doesn't have to be focused on fixing someone else but rather on supporting him as the person heals. "The strongest relationships," I've discovered, "are not the ones with no struggles, but ones that both of the partners are determined not to let go of one another. "

Supportive Husband

I will always remember the day when all things changed. It wasn't because of a grand love gesture but rather because of something as small as one moment of silence around the table in the kitchen. "I see you trying," the man stated, his hands over my hand. It was only five words, but they were all I required to be able to. He told me that I was not all on my own, that my work was necessary, and that we all were on the same page. That was the moment I realized what genuine love felt like. Not one that asks for thanks, but rather the kind that makes you feel loved and respected.

The relationship we had could have been better, as no relationship is ever perfect. However, what was unique about it was the method we used to put the relationship together. Word by word, brick-in-word, joys as well as tears built an unbreakable bond. It was more than just love; *the bond was one of bond that was based on confidence, respect, and development.* I wasn't aware of the magnitude of the relationship we shared until I started to look at it from the perspective of emotional security and intelligence.

One of the things I was taught was the value of feeling at ease, not just with my partner but within myself. At first, I struggled with self-doubt and was constantly unsure whether I had enough. His constant presence allowed me to put aside my doubts. He would remind me, "It's okay to be vulnerable. You don't have to have it all together." It was a remarkable aspect of our relationship, and it didn't revolve around one of us being a strong person every day; it was about helping each other out in times when we felt vulnerable.

Secure attachment has taught us to be completely trusting of one another. I could tell that when he said, *"I've got you,"* it was a true statement. Also, I was referring to it when I made the same statement. We were not afraid of being independent either. He pushed me to follow my interests, even if it involved late nights and early mornings with no one else. *"You're not just my partner,"* he would tell me. *"You're my inspiration. "* These words provided me with the confidence to imagine bigger dreams and know that I was supported by someone who believed in my abilities.

What I've discovered isn't only about butterflies or fireworks. It's about daily gestures of affection that say, *"You matter. "* A few nights ago, in the middle of a long and challenging day at work, I returned home and found a platter of my favourite food sitting at the table. The man didn't speak much; he just offered me a blanket and let me rest in silence. Then I realized it's not always quiet. Sometimes, it's calm and subtle, as in how he'd write notes inside my lunch box or how I'd stay up all night to review his presentation.

It wasn't only about showing up for one another when times were good; it was about being there in the tough times as well. If I lost someone close to me, my father didn't attempt to solve the issue. He held me and told me, *"Take all the time you need. "* These experiences made me realize that love isn't just about solving issues; it's about being together in the challenges.

Respect was the thread that binds us. It was not just about telling each other" Please*"* and *"thank you"* (though we also did those). The main thing was to appreciate our thoughts, emotions, and dreams truly. The rule was that we would never undermine each other's views, no matter how much we did not agree. "I may not see it the same way," said he, "but I'll always try to get my head around. "

One of the most vital instances of respect we have within our marriage was one of the most critical decisions in our lives. I was tempted to go back to school for business. However, I was afraid of the negative impact it might have on our relationship. Instead of viewing it as a burden, He believed it was an opportunity for each of us. *"Your growth is our growth,"* the man declared. He was serious about it. He changed his work timetable, added on household responsibilities, and encouraged me throughout the process. The kind of respect he showed me, the kind that tells me, *"Your dreams are as important as mine"*-- is what helped us grow more resilient.

One of the main lessons we learned was that progress doesn't happen in the same way or the same direction. And it's okay. There were instances when I thought I was running when I was walking. And there were moments when he seemed to be flying, and I was struggling to find my wings. Instead of letting these divergences impede our relationship, we used these differences to gain knowledge and learn from each other.

In the case of a friend, if He decided to begin a new company, it meant a long working day and nights of sleeplessness. In the beginning, I felt like a stranger, as if I didn't belong in his life any longer. However, I realized that the act of supporting him wasn't about being active in all things; it was about cheering on the sidelines and praising his wins just as if they were my own. As a result, he did similar things for me when I was pursuing my dreams. *"I'm proud of you,"* the man would declare, and I was sure that he was referring to me.

Every relationship is challenged, and we were no exception. What made our relationship different was the way we dealt with them, not in a way of battling but rather as partners. The most challenging moment was when he lost his job. It was a sigh of relief, and instead of having it split us, we took on this with one another. *"We'll figure this out,"* I assured me, and I meant that. We got together, came up with an outline, and reminded one another about our strengths. This wasn't an easy task, but it helped us get closer.

The other time, I needed help. I was overwhelmed by work, overwhelmed by the pressure of deadlines and doubts about myself. I'll never forget when he showed up unexpectedly with a cup of coffee and a motivational speech. *"You're not alone,"* He declared, and his words lifted me from a burden I did not even know I carried.

Suppose there's something that bonded us, that was our emotional intelligence. We were able to discern not only our emotions but also each other's. If I got angry, He didn't inquire, "What's wrong?" Then he would ask, *"How can I help? "* Also, whenever he felt stressed, I never pushed him to speak. I let him be until he was at ease.

Empathy was our new powerhouse. It was a matter of practicing active listening and being able to listen instead of waiting to react. The process wasn't always flawless--there was a time when our frustrations were a factor, but we stayed on the base we had built: *a commitment to being able to listen, not only respond.*

The thing I wasn't aware of until later was the extent to which the love we shared echoed throughout all other aspects of our lives. Since we bonded in such a way, we became healthier, happier people. This happiness is filtered through our relationships, work, and overall well-being. Many people would ask, *"What's your secret? "* The truth was that there was no secret. The main thing was to show that we were there for ourselves, our friends, and the lives we had built together.

If I can think of one thing that I've learned from my experience, it's that the love of your life isn't only about getting the perfect partner; it's about finding the ideal partner. It's about working on compassion, patience, and respect throughout the day. The goal is to celebrate each other's successes, however tiny, and put your best foot forward throughout each hurricane. The goal is to create a place that allows you to improve, not only individually but as part of a team.

In looking back at our lives, I see that *the love of my life is just a million tiny choices that have been made throughout many years*. The choices you make can make the most significant difference.

It's an affirmation of the power of love that is supportive, as well as a reminder that the best relationships are created and not simply created. Every word, every moment, or gesture establishes a bond that can stand up to whatever the world puts in your path.

Divergent Lifestyle

Life mirrors the complex nature of our relationships. It is a beautiful tapestry that weaves with threads of harmony as well as tension. The sky is a welcoming place for the moon and sun as two opposing forces that live together with each other, the one shining light on the day while creating peace in the dark. As rivers weave their way into stone, the differences between individuals shape the contours of connection, not by eliminating but rather by accepting the conflict between flow and resistance.

An introverted person can experience the calmness of a lake. An extrovert has a dance like the sunlight shining onto the lake's surface. Together, they create an entire, with energy and reflection interspersed. The solid earth and unpredictable winds might seem to be at odds, but they are a part of each other and create life.

In the words of Rumi, *"Out beyond ideas of wrongdoing and right-doing, there is a field. I'll meet you there. "* In relations, that field can be located in the ability to be open, listen, and embrace differences, as well as being aware that unity doesn't refer to the sameness of a person but rather the ability to be genuinely different in a group.

A Source of Conflict or Growth?

Our values and our personalities define the complex tapestry of our relationships, weaving together strength and vulnerability into each interaction. Intimacy interactions are not about perfection but rather about harmony. Two worlds meet by way of their respective traditions, which dance between different perspectives. According to Rainer Maria Rilke wrote: *"For one human being to love another: that is perhaps the most difficult of all our tasks."* It is a matter of determination to accept the imperfections as well as the beautiful aspects of each other by creating a place to develop. The ones who take on this challenge find that love isn't so much about finding the ideal companion but more about becoming an integral part of each other.

The Emotional Rift: Thinkers and Feelers

They are so solid and fragile that they can connect us or tear us. In relationships, our emotional processing patterns often dictate the way we interact during conflicts. For those who think logic can be a way to escape. For feelers, compassion is the way to go. I have a close friend who told me about a particularly traumatic dispute with her co-worker. She was crying out her feelings in a vulnerable and raw way but then was told, *"Let's focus on fixing the problem. "* That was the moment when she wasn't looking for a solution but desired compassion.

To those with a mind, emotions appear hazy and uncertain, while feelers might view the logic of detachment as cold. The disconnect can create an emotional vacuum. It is a place where vulnerability can be substituted by anger. If unchecked, the vacuum is an ideal place for infidelity. When one person feels left out or disregarded, they could need to seek out emotional approval in another place.

However, there's hope. The process of growth begins when people recognize the value of emotions and those who feel understand the precision of reason. The goal isn't to abandon your nature but instead to become able to communicate with the language of others. People who think about it can ask, *"What does my partner need emotionally right now?"* People who feel like they can explore, *"How can I present my feelings in a way my partner will understand?"* By bridging this gap in emotions and building not just confidence but also resilience.

Values: The Unseen Foundations

In every struggle lies the truth behind beliefs. They're not visible, yet they're everywhere, impacting the way we behave, live, and even dream. Imagine a partner who is devoted to the pursuit of self-discovery and growth, always striving to discover new possibilities. The other is content with the stability of tradition. While neither is correct, the different views of each can cause friction, especially when important decisions come up.

What happens if these values aren't compatible? A couple may feel that their desires are not being considered, and the other is the pressure to alter who they have become. This gap will grow, and infidelity can become a means to find their sense of what's not being fulfilled. However, before the fracture gets any more severe, couples should ask, *"How can we honour each other's values?"*

The solution lies in the balance. The issue isn't about one of the partners giving up their goals but rather being able to work together and support one another. The stability-seeking spouse might offer assistance during the transition of their career, and the one who is looking for growth discovers the value of remaining consistent when the values of both parties align or in a situation where differences are acknowledged love blossoms.

The Daily Grind: Routines and Resentment

There's always a risk in living a monotonous life. In time, the excitement of romance can turn into routines that can feel oppressive. Some partners may start to desire liberation, whereas another relies on rituals for a sense of security. I've heard about a couple who, over time, drifted to the point that they were living different lives. The couple wasn't cruel or unloving, and yet they ceased to grow in their relationship. *The silence became an ideal place for infidelity, not from the absence of love; however, it was due to a lack of connections.*

There is no need to break away from routines; instead, we should establish rituals that strengthen the bond. Making a meal with your partner, walking together during sunset, or having the same cup of tea can be acts of love. These are moments that remind us that affection isn't only about grand gestures; it's all in the simple, deliberate ways of showing love to the other.

The Danger of Silence: Infidelity's Breeding Ground

It can be a comforting feeling to hear silence, but it can also cause a lot of damage. When partners stop communicating--whether out of fear, frustration, or fatigue--misunderstandings multiply. Someone who is feeling ignored might begin to seek the attention of someone else not simply because they do not love their spouse but rather because they feel unimportant. *It's not just about the desire to be loved but rather about a lack of satisfaction.*

Building trust in silence requires opening up communication channels. This is about asking difficult questions, expressing fears and listening with a sincere heart. *Only when we break the silence can couples begin to recover.*

In its essence, the act of loving requires bravery. It's about accepting the differences in others and deciding to view these differences not as obstacles but instead as potential opportunities to grow. True compatibility does not mean finding people who are like us, but it involves finding someone who challenges us and makes us better. Philosopher Alain de Botton wrote, *"Compatibility is an achievement of love; it must not be its precondition."*

Infidelity is a topic that does not have to be concluded in a finale. It's a gruelling yet transformative time by addressing needs that aren't being met in addition to the underlying issues that led to break-ups and the need to build a strong base. When you're willing to confront the challenges of loving one another, every comment is a chance to improve your relationships. The appeal of a love marriage isn't in its perfection; it lies in the power.

Navigating Divergent Paths

Harmony in relationships is a complex dance of a sense of belonging and harmony in which respect for differences enhances the everyday experience. Studies from Harvard's Study of Adult Development, which spans over eighty years, revealed that healthy relationships are *built on mutual respect and curiosity about the inner lives of each other. A partner who acknowledges and does not suppress their differences is more satisfied and has greater resilience.*

Philosophically, this harmony is similar to Khalil Gibran's quote: *"Let there be spaces in your togetherness."* Spaces like this allow for diverse thinking, which allows for the exploration of infinite possibilities to join converging thinking. This is where a common thread emerges. It strengthens relationships that create a bond that grows rather than becoming stagnant.

Relationships are enriched in a world where individuality is not seen as a problem but rather as an asset. Recognizing that we're different but interconnected is a reflection of nature, like rivers merging into the ocean's vast expanse, each one retaining its essence but being a part of the overall.

In embracing the diversity of ideas and beliefs, friendships go beyond mere coexistence and create an environment in which individuality can breathe freely while uniting grows.

Divergent Love - The Clash of Lifestyles

"Show me how you live, and I'll see who you are." The profound message resonates strongly, particularly in the delicate and complex web of human interactions. How we live our lives is more than an accumulation of routines; it's an expression of our values. Our beliefs at the core are a mirror that reflects the core beliefs that we hold dear. If two individuals have compatible lifestyles, it establishes an understanding of rhythm and trust, forming intimacy's basis.

Consider the person who begins the day with a sense of thoughts and contemplation, enjoying peace, and contrasted with someone awed by late-night bustle. They aren't simply routines; they're profound statements of the values that each value--delight versus peace and stability against spontaneity. If these values align and are in harmony, there's less space for confusion and less room for doubt to invade.

Infidelity can be found due to a lack of connection and unshared values. If partners lead lifestyles that reflect shared values, they can create trust and lessen the psychological distance that can cause being betrayed. Sharing an everyday lifestyle does more than provide companionship; it is also an intricate web of Respect and loyalty.

"When two lives take separate paths yet choose to walk together, their differences become the lessons that teach patience, compassion, and resilience. "

Real World Implication

The art of love has a method of connecting some of the most surprising pairings and weaving stories that are full of contradictions, struggles, and development. This story is a prime example of the many contrasts. It is a tale of two lives colliding and not fitting well, but instead as sharp edges trying to discover an agreement. However, amid these divergences, we found that relationships are not based on similarities but on patience, understanding, and mutual Respect.

The contrasts were enchanting in the first few minutes of our trip as if being in an ocular. I was a meticulous planner who liked the order of things and a routine. My companion? He was impulsive and a natural, elusive butterfly, seeking pleasure wherever it took. The rhythms of our lives clashed, but they were also in sync. The spontaneity of his personality pushed me from my comfortable area, and my structure gave him the foundation he secretly wanted. The two of us were at odds, but the differences between us in the beginning created peace.

A particular instance that sticks out was when he opted in the middle of nowhere to take us for a trip on the road without any plan. I was shocked for someone who carefully plans travel plans down to the final minute detail. But the trip that was not planned was one of the most unforgettable memories of my lifetime, filled with surprises, unplanned adventures, and a profound realization that not everything has to be planned to enjoy the experience. However, when his spontaneity caused him to miss a date for an important assignment, my routine of keeping a meticulous calendar helped me get through the day. This experience reinforced that we were not rivals fighting for supremacy. We were all parts of a larger picture, and each one filled in the other's gaps.

With time, however, those differences, which were once so exciting, began to cause tension. It wasn't the differences that were the problem; it was how we dealt with them. When I was in a heated argument with my partner, I told myself that he didn't appreciate the effort I put into planning our weekends. It was a raw but instructive response: *"It isn't that I do not value your efforts; sometimes your plans make me feel like there is no space to breathe."*

In the same way, he was annoyed by my dismissal of his need to be flexible as a sign of irresponsibility. In my efforts to mould him into a person who reflected my expectations and my expectations, I had stifled the essence of what attracted me to him initially: his exuberant nature. The tension-filled moments brought to light a crucial reality: differences could create or hinder the relationship, contingent on how they are dealt with.

The pivotal moment came in an incredibly vulnerable conversation. Both of us shared our anxieties and fears. "Your structure isn't a burden," the man admitted, "but sometimes it feels like there's no room for my ideas." In the same way, I confessed to him, "Your spontaneity scares me because it feels unpredictable, and I find comfort in knowing what's coming." It was a painful confession; however, it was the start of an increased knowledge.

As time passed, we created strategies that suited both our requirements. When making plans for vacations, we began mixing our different styles. I would sketch out the main places and logistical details, and he would choose informal activities like walking in local markets or seeking out obscure routes. Our compromises let us achieve an atmosphere where we were respected and heard.

Our daily routines We established little rituals to make the gaps. The boy began using a whiteboard in the kitchen, where he would write down random thoughts, giving me stability and a more free-spirited attitude. For my part, I began to leave spaces in my routine, leaving room for his spontaneous excursions. These small changes are crucial and reinforce the notion that love shouldn't be about eliminating the differences but instead making them a more cohesive relationship.

Open communication was the basis of our relationship. We began asking each other, *"Why do you feel this way?"* instead of being apprehensive. When I was frustrated by his inability to commit to the future, he clarified the reason for his hesitation as an anxiety about losing his identity and not from a lack of affection towards me. In the same way, he realized that my adoration for structures wasn't about controlling them but rather about establishing a solid base for us all.

"Love isn't about eliminating differences; it's about growing together without shrinking each other." These words, which we shared during a therapy session, came to be our mantra. We were reminded that the individuality we have was not a danger to our relationships but an asset we could use.

The most transformational moment occurred months later after we began building. I was surprised by his plan for an evening out at my favourite eatery, with an agenda written in hand. It was a gesture that was a testament to his determination to meet me at my level. When I returned, I accompanied the two on a hike he had not planned the following morning, accepting the uncertainties of the day. These small gestures of kindness were powerful and rekindled the fire that brought us together at first.

Another illustration of this dynamic was when we discussed beginning the family. As much as I viewed children as an inevitable next step, my husband was worried about losing his sense of freedom. Instead of allowing this to become an argument and a source of contention, we tackled it in a group. Through many conversations, we came to accept each other's viewpoints while agreeing to revisit this issue when at the same level.

The journey we took with us taught us valuable lessons.

1. Instead of seeing our differences as barriers, we see the differences as strengths. The spontaneity of his personality helped me appreciate all the charm of this moment. Meanwhile, my structures helped him stay grounded through the turbulent moments.

2. Rebuilding trust and getting to a place of harmony requires patience. There were times of discontent and failure, but every move strengthened us.

3. Love can only flourish when both parties are respected and valued. When we respect each other's wants and needs, we build a basis of trust and gratitude.

Divergent love can be practical as it pushes us to develop. We are forced to face our fears, accept different perspectives, and come up with new ways to resolve conflicts. The goal is not to change the person we're currently but to dance to the rhythm of each other, no matter if it feels like the steps aren't familiar.

According to the words of the writer Alain de Botton:

"Compatibility is an achievement of love; it must not be its precondition." Our differences didn't hurt our bond, but they enriched it by strengthening us, making us more empathic and aware of each other's needs.

Our relationship today isn't ideal, nor should it ever be. While we celebrate our successes and make mistakes, we're still negotiating the delicate balance. We've learned that loving someone doesn't mean sharing similar traits. Accepting the beautiful diversity in our differences is about finding joy and delight in the unexpected. It is also about collaborating with others, not letting go, and not giving up.

In a culture that considers love to be the same thing, our story stands as an example of the strength of divergence. This story reminds us that real love doesn't have to be about looking perfect to each other. It's about creating a bond that is so strong that even the most sharp edges will find ways to be a part of each other.

The Power of Shared Habits

"Love is not measured in grand gestures but in the quiet consistency of showing up daily," Someone once stated. And nowhere is this truer than in the world of routines. Shared goals do not base the foundation of relationships but also on simple, non-verbal agreements that form the basis of a couple's everyday routine. How two individuals manage their lives--the routines they follow in the morning and the pace they prefer for their evenings or the tempo of their conversations can either create an intricate web of connections or lead to discord. Once couples can align their lives, they can allow for more understanding. Love is a result of everyday activities, including a night out.

"Love thrives in the spaces between grand gestures; it is nourished by the consistency of shared habits and the comfort of knowing someone is always there."

Real World Implication

The path to infidelity is often not through a single, devastating incident or a single act but rather a sequence of misplaced events and tiny gaps in the foundations of a marriage. The betrayal isn't the only thing that causes trust to be destroyed and trust, but rather the feeling of isolation that has gotten between the cracks and gone unnoticed or spoken. A solution to this separation? Sharing routines. These are the skeleton that keeps love strong, even when things seem slightly off.

Shared habits are the invisible threads that weave intimacy in everyday life. They provide opportunities to bond, to be present, and to keep each other in mind: *"I see you. I'm choosing for you."* If these routines are not followed, the bonds of friendship become vulnerable. Imagine a couple who once formed bonds by having an evening dinner together. In time, their ritual is ruined into take-out containers behind separate screens. The space is left unattended, and disconnection is a common occurrence.

If shared routines are lost, the couples can be two islands without a bridge. This is the place where infidelity may be able to flourish, not because the love of one has gone away and the bond is a snare.

One of my friends once said to me, *"Infidelity thrives where intimacy is forgotten."* The intimacy isn't just physical; it's also emotional. Small or no habits make a place that allows intimacy to thrive.

The moment I learned of the deceit seemed like a rumbling earthquake. The world I created together with a person I was devoted to seemed to fall apart, leaving fragments of trust on my floor. I sought answers in the chaos:

How did this occur?

What caused us to drift to this point?

Hurt constantly sought explanations for the brokenness in a relationship I used to believe was indestructible.

The lessons I gleaned in the following days were transformative. It was clear that infidelity does not necessarily result from an isolated act. It is more likely to manifest without connection by losing daily routines that unite two souls. These small routines--joking over morning coffee, discussing the day with the other's life, or taking a walk together walk -- had all but disappeared. The loneliness swept in in their absence, unblocking an unintentional door that shouldn't be opened.

In the chaos, I could hold onto the tiniest spark of hope: *Habits are the foundation of our love.* I recollected to myself. If the demise of these rituals led us to this point, maybe their return could help us get to the past.

The first step towards healing was the easy action of sharing mornings. The process began awkwardly and even slowly. We decided to welcome one another every morning with a hug and an unspoken "I love you." Breakfast was shared, and we resisted the routine of checking phones with no one else. Initially, we struggled in conversation, not knowing which words to use. Over time, however, those times were transformed into sacred.

"It's not just the coffee," I informed him in the morning. *"It's the time to pause. It's deciding to be with each other before the chaotic day."*

Through these small actions, I could begin seeing the man I'd fallen in love with. The walls between us started to fall.

In the evening, we began the practice we call *the Listening Hour*. Every week, for an hour, it was a time to put away everything else--no phones, no other distractions or TVs--and speak. It wasn't about resolving issues or revisiting old wounds but listening.

When we first met, I asked him a straightforward question: *"Tell me one thing you're grateful for today."* He hesitated but finally declared a minor victory at his job. His voice was filled with emotion I hadn't heard for an extended time: vulnerability.

Each week, the conversations have become a place of refuge. We jokingly shared our dreams and shared worries. Being recognized, of being noticed, started to restore the faith we believed we'd lost.

On the advice of a close friend, we set out to create an area of our own. *"Build something," she told us, "And watch it grow."* We both have green thumbs, and initially, the concept was a bit ridiculous. However, as we dug our teeth into the dirt, there was a shift.

This garden evolved into more than just a place to grow plants; it was also a metaphor for our friendship. Every seedling we nurtured proved the value of cooperation, perseverance, and a shared effort. Every new seed seemed like a little victory -- a sign of hope growing.

One of the most challenging behaviours to tackle was our dependence on computers. Technology was a way to escape from reality, an opportunity to stay clear of awkward conversations.

"What if we made dinner sacred?" I proposed an evening.

We also banned television and phones at the dining room table. The silence at first was deafening. However, it was soon filled with laughter, stories, and the clanking of plates. As time passed, this easy gesture of being completely present turned our evenings into beloved connecting rituals.

"Distraction is the enemy of intimacy," I discovered. In choosing to connect over our gadgets, we built a bridge that was frayed.

Rebuilding following a loss requires more than actions. It calls for a change of mindset. To forgive, I realized it's not a one-time act but a routine of surrendering, day in and minute.

There were times when my anger grew and threatened to sabotage our accomplishments. In those situations, I repeated the affirmation: *Choose love over the pain.*

Instead of yelling and ranting, I wrote letters expressing my pain, worries, and optimism. The letters were a means to manage my feelings and not let them impede our growth. As time passed, forgiveness became an everyday decision to prioritize healing over anger.

The power of shared habits is establishing a base of trust and connection. They can be the solution to loneliness and isolation. Coffee in the morning, time spent listening, gardening, and dinners without screens might seem insignificant, but their effects are profound.

Every ritual strengthened our bonds, which made room for anxiety or feeling lonely. These events were the glue that kept us all together despite difficulties.

"Love isn't grand gestures; it's showing up every day," I am reminded in the morning cup of coffee.

It was through the universality of our routines that we came to know each other again.

There have been many years since that night when trust was breached. In retrospect, I do not consider the incident to be an end to our story but rather a turning point.

Our new routines not only saved our relationship but transformed it. Every meal shared, every quiet conversation, and every minute of being present has become a win.

The love I've come to think that it isn't an isolated feeling or an extravagant gesture. It's a choice that you make every day. The way we live our lives is in the patterns we develop, the routines we keep, and our presence to one another.

As long as we keep choosing one another day or habit after habit, I am confident that we can weather any storm.

"Habits," I've discovered, "are the language of love."

Finding Common Ground in Purpose

Vision alignment is the constant pulse in relationships that keeps love in motion. It's not about firmly combining two lives. Instead, it's about weaving your dreamscapes into a beautiful tapestry of common purpose. Imagine two people in the same space, under the same sky, each dreaming differently but hugging each other and saying, *"I don't need to search elsewhere because my dreams already feel complete with you."* It's not just an expression of love but the basis for a long-lasting relationship. Achieving vision alignment isn't simply a matter of ideals and the pathway toward unity, happiness, and unshakeable trust.

"When your dreams find their rhythm in another's purpose, love becomes the bridge between two worlds."

Real World Implication

As I look back on our (me and my partner) lives together, one of the most profound lessons we have learned has been realizing the power of aligning our visions. At first, our differences felt like barriers. I was looking forward to building a startup, writing books, and getting an appreciation for my work; however, my partner wanted to dedicate her life to social service, meditation, and making an actual change in people's lives. Initially, our objectives appeared to be completely different, but when we sifted through the layers of our lives, we discovered the extent to which they are interconnected.

At first, these differences caused disagreement. *"Why can't you see that building a business can help others?"* I'd claim, and my partner will counter, *"Not everything has to be about financial success in terms of society. The real impact is in Being present and sharing.* "These conversations not only frustrated us but were emotionally exhausting. We both feared that our diverging pathways could lead us into a rift.

A breakthrough occurred in a peaceful evening, in which I asked, *"What does success mean to you?"* This was an important question I should have asked long ago. My partner's response shocked me: *"Success is creating peace and helping others see their worth."* Then, I noticed a significant connection between our goals. My dreams of entrepreneurship could complement my desire to help others. Two perspectives were working towards the same goal.

Then, we began to transform our arguments into plans for collaboration. In particular, I started looking at how my partner's need for mindfulness might influence my ventures in business. I considered incorporating social causes in my business ventures, like allocating a certain percentage of the profits to local programs and hosting retreats for mindfulness. My partner advised me to document these efforts, which gave me an authentic approach to merging my voices with theirs.

An example of this was our project: A digital platform that aims to give back to communities in need. I managed marketing and business strategies while my coworker concentrated on creating wellness classes and meditation guides. The way we complemented one another was incredibly satisfying. *"Your determination inspires me to act,"* my partner once said. I responded, *"And your perspective grounds me."*

When our relationship grew more robust, it created an impact on our relationship. Our communication became more freely, even on challenging issues. It helped build trust and made it less likely for anxiety to get a foothold. We realized that infidelity is often rooted in unsatisfied emotional needs or feelings that there is a disconnect. When we began to develop the foundation of a common purpose that became an anchor, we realized that we were all doing this as a team and were striving to achieve something bigger beyond ourselves.

Let me tell you about when I was overwhelmed by an unsettling business decision. Instead of providing suggestions, my partner suggested, *"Let's meditate on it."* In the beginning, I was hesitant, as it seemed unpractical. However, as we sat down together, I experienced a clarity I had never experienced before. Similar to when my partner had doubts about the effects of social work, I encouraged her to believe in the impact of her work by telling stories of life-changing experiences resulting from our joint actions. *"You have no idea how many people you've touched,"* I told her.

Achieving alignment with your vision does not mean you have to lose your personal identity; instead, it's about aligning your strengths to make something more significant. Nowadays, I consider the divergent perspectives of my partner not as barriers but as opportunities that strengthen our relationship. *"We're not competing with each other,"* my partner previously said. *"We're building something together."*

As a result of this awareness, I've discovered deep calm. Being aware that my companion is trying to reach the same destination with their unique perspective can be deeply comfortable, like having a friend who is always looking over your blind spots as you look over theirs. While working towards our common goals, I'm confident this collaboration has strengthened our bond in ways I had never thought of.

Can Opposites Truly Attract?

Opposites attract relationships and can bring great harmony and transformation. Take, for example, a relationship between a risk-taking entrepreneur and a cautious financial planner or a relationship between a free-spirited artist and a structured engineer. Initially, these may appear like 'fire and ice.' Yet, both individuals can benefit from understanding each other's qualities, where one thrives off risk and creativity while their counterpart thrives through structure and planning.

Contrast is at the core of identity; through empathy and open communication, individuals can understand each other's perspectives to bridge differences between their personalities. Carl Jung observed: *'When two personalities meet, it is like meeting two chemical substances: any interaction transforms both.'* By accepting each other's ways, both partners may become stronger - perhaps one learns spontaneity while the other finds peace through reflection - creating not simply transformation through understanding but an exciting shared journey! This emphasis on empathy and communication can reassure and instill confidence in the audience about the potential of their relationships.

"When opposites collide, they don't destroy; they ignite the fire of transformation."

Real World Implication

It's hilarious how things unfold in a way. You're within your perfect life, all arranged by neat little boxes and timelines, but then, the next moment, a stranger enters your world like a storm of chaos and colour. It was precisely how it happened to me. It was a collision between two extremes that were so stark it seemed like a cosmic slap in the role of a game.

I was a fan of the order. Planned activities gave me the purpose I needed, the structure gave me peace, and certainty was my most excellent companion. I used spreadsheets to plan my vacations and a color-coded calendar to track every job and list - oh, the lists! My days were like symphonies that were orchestrated with accuracy and precision.

Then, the storm. Insane, unpredictable, and erratic, He swept through my world, challenging every thought I had made. He saw the concept of schedules as a cage and spontaneity as a way to be free. This was harrowing for me, who thrived on knowing what was coming next. "Why can't you stick to the plan?" I'd beg. He'd laugh, smile, and then whisk me away for an unplanned night drive, dancing through the drizzle or enjoying the night without plans.

It was initially difficult. The pull and push between us were overwhelming, like trying to mix oil with water. In all the confusion, something changed. I recall when we had no plans, and I tentatively said, *"Just see where the evening takes us."* The evening that transpired was awe-inspiring: laughter, surprise discovery, and experiences I'd never put into a plan. The realization hit me then: Life wasn't designed to be managed entirely. Sometimes, the most memorable memories come from the ones that aren't planned.

However, he began to find comfort in my provided structure. The first few days were difficult as he didn't like sticking to a plan or adhering to a routine. When I could help him plan his goals--things he'd thought about but ended up putting off, he realized how important it was to the balance. *"It feels good to know what's ahead. "I'd* ask. As he progressed, he began making spaces for peace in the chaos, discovering that structure wasn't hindering his life's spontaneity but instead facilitated spontaneity.

It wasn't easy, but it was full of obstacles. At times, I would retreat from the chaos, overwhelmed by his restless energy and feeling that I'd lost my sense of stability. On other days, he'd withdraw, irritated at what he viewed as my stifling. In those instances, we learned the importance of communicating, not just talking but listening.

I came across a quote that stuck for me to this day: "Understanding is love in its purest form." This became our motto. Instead of trying to alter our relationship, we started to get to know each other. I realized that his spontaneity was not an absence of discipline but a method of living life to the fullest. He recognized that the need to structure in me wasn't concerned with control but rather being able to find peace in a chaotic life.

The feelers and the thinkers are caught within this dance. My logic-driven side frequently clashed with his emotional understanding. I approached challenges as if he were problems to be solved, whereas he wanted to feel emotions, examine his feelings, and acknowledge them. I would become impatient and look for answers, and he would become frustrated seeking connection instead of resolution.

However, we did discover an opening. It taught me that it's not always necessary to fix everything. Sometimes, emotions need room to function. And in return, I demonstrated to him how stepping back and looking at things from a different perspective can empower him. This wasn't about letting go of the person we are but growing into the person we can become.

Social interactions, too, are a thrill. Being an introvert, I loved quiet times by myself, taking a break with a book or long conversations. The extroverts, by nature, flourished during lively gatherings, with their enthusiasm exploding with each encounter. The first time, it seemed as though there were a few more divisions. Then, we realized the value of the concept of compromise. I started to appreciate the excitement of his world in which socializing was not draining but rather an opportunity to experience new things. In turn, he discovered peace and tranquillity, taking in the tranquil moments that had always been my place of refuge.

It was clear that love doesn't have to be about getting rid of differences but instead making him into a seamless tapestry that allows space between the two people. Our quirks that were previously points to be fought over turned out to be our most beloved traits. The most in one another. The spontaneity of his interactions reminded me to surrender and let go in the moment, and my structure helped him to find the basis to fly.

Sometimes, it wasn't easy, but it was worth the effort. When we worked through our disagreements and rediscovered something important, our relationship was not about letting ourselves go to one another but finding the person we are. Our relationship grew as individuals, and we gained the ability to appreciate parts of ourselves that we had previously ignored.

The bottom line is that opposing forces don't simply attract; they alter. He tests and annoys us, and if you let him help us learn. He teaches us that love isn't just about being alike; it's about the ability to cross boundaries and to be able to endure the difficulty of differences and find peace and harmony, not by erasing differences instead of honouring these differences.

In retrospect, our strength wasn't that we were alike but rather in taking the time to share our knowledge. We created something unique, not because of our differences but our differences. "You don't complete me," he'd say often, "but you make me whole." Isn't that a beautiful type of love?

The Journey to Compatibility

The bond between people goes far past physical looks. It is about acknowledging and recognizing each person's individuality. Traits can strengthen understanding, strength and understanding that improve friendships.

"The Journey to Compatibility" prove that genuine compatibility is more than acknowledging similarities but understanding the diverse views of people. This fascinating journey focuses on the delight of diversity and builds connections by recognizing unique qualities as opportunities for growth. This trip will strengthen bonds because it acknowledges that differences provide opportunities to grow and learn while accepting differences as an element of the process. This can help strengthen the bonds between

Are you looking for love or a Relationship? For the relationship to succeed, each partner must work to improve communication and understanding of one another in their individuality. An enduring relationship that demonstrates mutual respect. This ensures that harmony isn't created by a stale way of thinking but rather by being able to see the different views. This is a must when both parties want to attain happiness.

Diverse Perspectives as Catalysts for Growth

Think about a couple where one individual thrives on excitement while another seeks ease in routine; from a first impression, they may appear as challenges. But looking at them with a philosophical eye becomes an opportunity to develop. A spontaneous person learns the importance of planning, and the one who is structured can experience the pleasures of uncertainty.

Personalized Relationship Dynamics

As we grew closer, it often felt like we resided on opposing sides of the spectrum. We both adored the excitement of spontaneity. However, the other was content with routine. The evenings we shared mirrored this difference. One might think of a spontaneous journey, whereas others adored the peaceful peace of reading a book before the fireplace.

Our differing opinions were not barriers but rather bridges. There were times when the adventure-seeker recommended a last-minute weekend excursion. At first, the comfortable person resisted the thought of the lack of preparation. The hike was an experience of complete connection, excitement, and discovery. The adventurer started recognizing the value of a quiet evening in the present, increasing our bonds.

This balanced perspective reduced the possibility of miscommunication, increased our confidence, and naturally slowed down any potential for unfaithfulness. In embracing our strengths, We created a shared goal: being supportive, understanding, and growing. Psychotherapist Esther Perel states, *"The quality of your relationships determines the quality of your life."* Experiences shared and rooted in respect for each other are the basis for fidelity.

Our growth was by way of small and intimate compromises. The quote we are most comfortable with is, *"We don't see things as they are; we see them as we are"* (Anais Nin). Recognizing this, we have redefined disputes not as conflict but as learning opportunities. Today, we enjoy both the adventure of discovering something unfamiliar and the pleasure of being familiar.

We came to peace in our journey together when we embraced our different perspectives. Growing and connecting isn't just about eliminating differences but creating something unique to our own. We've created an environment where trust is cultivated, and love has a feeling of being infinite.

Narrating Perspectives: Compatibility In Diverse Viewpoints

The Spontaneous Getaway

Me: "How about we pack up and head to the mountains for the weekend? No plans, just us and nature!"
My Spouse: "Wait, what? Without reservations? What if we don't find a place to stay or run into trouble?"
Me: "That's the fun part! We'll figure it out as we go."
My Spouse: "Alright, let's try it. But I'm bringing a map, just in case."
Reflection: My spouse and I both learned that planning can be helpful but is only sometimes required.

Movie Night Decisions

Me: "Let's watch that new thriller that just came out. It'll be so exciting!"

My Spouse: "How about a feel-good rom-com? I've had a long day and need something relaxing."

Me: "You know what? Let's flip a coin. And no matter what, we'll try to enjoy it together."

Reflection: We laughed and were reminded to compromise, even on the smallest of things.

Dinner Plans Clash

My Spouse: "I've been looking forward to cooking that new recipe tonight. It's our little tradition to cook together on Fridays."

Me: "I was thinking we could go out for a surprise dinner instead. It's been a while since we tried something new."

My Spouse: "What if we cook tonight and plan a surprise dinner for next Friday?"

Me: "Deal! But you have to let me pick the restaurant next week."

Reflection: We valued both spontaneities, and our routines by alternating them.

Lazy Sunday Morning

Me: "Let's sleep in and have breakfast in bed today. No alarms, no rush!"

My Spouse: "Sounds amazing, but I was hoping to get an early start and explore the local farmer's market."

Me: "What if we sleep in, then head out later? A relaxed start and some adventure."

My Spouse: "Perfect. Let's do it!"

Reflection: We created shared moments of happiness by blending calmness and excitement on Sundays.

Future Planning

My Spouse: "I think we should start saving for a big vacation next year. Planning it out will help us budget and make the most of the experience."

Me: "That sounds great, but can we leave room for some spontaneous plans along the way? Like a surprise weekend getaway before the big trip?"

My Spouse: "Absolutely. Planning and spontaneity can go hand in hand."

Reflection: We realized together that long-term success doesn't require sacrificing moments of spontaneity and joy.

The Role of Empathy in Compatibility

Empathy plays an essential role in fostering understanding and building relationships. It allows people to put themselves on each other's feet and see the world from different perspectives without judgment. The empathetic way of thinking creates an environment where differences are acknowledged rather than resisted.

Personalized Relationship Dynamics

At one point, I believed that knowing someone's personality was as easy as knowing his preferences, interests, or what he sought. However, the world has a way of revealing just how complex human relationships are. Empathy -- truly feeling what another experiences--was not something that I regularly did until one particular event transformed my entire life.

Conflicts occur as a matter of course when you are at the beginning of a relationship. One particular one was noticeable: a constant fight with a matter that seemed so minor that it was ridiculous. But, every time the issue occurred, it escalated to something more significant. We debated, going over the same problems and talking to each other, not talking to one another. It was as if we had been speaking two languages, and neither was ready to give up.

In the evening, following another confrontation I could resolve, I consciously decided to stop instead of trying to defend my position and focusing on his conversation, not just his words, but the motivation behind his. While he talked, it became clear that he was revealing the threads in a bigger narrative. An incident from some time ago, well before our first meeting, affected his response to the present scenario. I'd never thought of that because I was not listening to my heart.

There was no way that I agreed with everything he said. Empathy doesn't mean letting go of the perspective you hold; it's about understanding the root of a person. I could see his struggles and suffering, and then, suddenly, it wasn't about whether or not it was correct but rather about resolving the issue together.

Such experiences have made me realise that empathy demands patience. There were moments when I required time to process his emotions, and I was tempted to try and find a solution. However, compatibility doesn't mean getting things done promptly. It's about extending patience when the other needs it. *"Sometimes the greatest gift we can give is our silence and our presence,"* I was once told, and this could not be more true.

Empathy changed the way we deal with our differences. The concept of compatibility changed from merely checking off shared interests to making an authentic bond. We can appreciate one another for who we are, not because of our differences but due to our differences.

The result is that genuine empathy can bridge the gap between people and turn disagreement into the mutual ability to understand and turn strangers into friends. We learn to listen not only to our ears but also to our hearts. In those instances, the feeling of love isn't something to choose, but it is a natural extension of knowing.

Narrating Perspectives: Compatibility In Empathy

The Forgotten Anniversary

Me: "I can't believe you forgot our anniversary. It feels like you don't care about us."

Spouse: "I'm so sorry. I've been overwhelmed with work deadlines and my mind has been all over the place."

Me: (pausing to reflect) "I see how much pressure you've been under lately. I guess I assumed anniversaries were as big of a deal for you as they are for me."

Spouse: "They are. I just didn't prioritize it the way I should have. Thank you for understanding. Let's plan something special for this weekend."

A Disagreement on Parenting Style

Me: "I think you're being too lenient with our child. They need discipline, or they'll never learn boundaries."

Spouse: "I hear you, but when I was a kid, strict rules made me feel suffocated. I want them to feel heard and safe, not scared of making mistakes."

Me: (after a moment of thought) "I didn't realize your childhood shaped your approach like that. Maybe we can find a middle ground that balances discipline with understanding."

Spouse: "I'd like that. Thanks for listening to where I'm coming from."

The Late-Night Work Call

Me: "You're always on your phone, even at dinner. I feel like I'm competing with your job for attention."

Spouse: "I know it seems like that, but this project has me stretched so thin. If I drop the ball now, my team will struggle, and I'll feel like I let everyone down."

Me: "That must be a lot of pressure. I don't want to add to your stress, but I also miss having you fully present."
Spouse: "I'll set clearer boundaries for work calls during dinner. Thanks for helping me see this from your perspective."

The Unexpected Emotional Reaction

Me: "Why are you so upset about something so small? I didn't mean anything by it."
Spouse: "It's not just about what you said. It brought up memories of being criticized constantly when I was younger."
Me: "I didn't realize how much that still affects you. I'm sorry for triggering that. I'll be more mindful of my words in the future."
Spouse: "Thank you. It's not easy for me to explain, but I feel better knowing you care enough to understand."

The Silent Treatment

Me: "You've been so quiet all evening. Did I do something wrong?"
Spouse: "No, it's not you. I had a rough day and feel drained. I just need some space to process everything."
Me: "Okay, I understand. I'll give you the time you need. Let me know if there's anything I can do to help."
Spouse: (later) "Thank you for being patient. Just knowing you're here helps more than you realize."

A Harmonious Coexistence

The path to harmony isn't about eliminating individuality but rather weaving distinct threads to form a unified whole when we recognise that differences do not pose obstacles but instead forces that complement each other that can bring harmony to relationships beyond superficial similarities.

Personalized Relationship Dynamics

In retrospect, I wasn't aware of how much I had clung to my view. It was safe at home, comfortable, and strangely encouraging to know that my method was correct. I was elated by my ability to make good decisions and navigate through difficulties using the instincts I believed were unquestionable. However, life, like it usually does, was not in my plans. Plans were wrapped up by the perspectives and voices of people around me, forcing me to rethink my assumptions about what I was taught.

At one point, disagreements felt like interruptions. The counterargument of a friend or partner's different approach seemed like obstructions to conquer rather than opening doors. I can remember one particular moment when I was working on a project that was a life-changing experience for me. I believed I'd considered everything and meticulously made every decision. However, my chest became tense and angry when a coworker was sceptical of my approach. What was the reason they couldn't believe in me?

However, their comments lingered. *"Have you considered this from another angle?"* The question seemed simple and gentle, yet it challenged my self-confidence in ways I could not overcome. The first time, I tried to resist. I kept pushing forward to prove that I was correct. The work progressed, and as problems began to appear, I noticed myself replaying the question inside my head. I realized my desire to stick to my track had obliterated me from a better solution.

The issue was related to more than work. Regarding my relationships, I began to realise my reliance on the false sense of certainty. During a dispute, one of my friends once said, *"I'm not trying to fight you--I'm trying to understand you."* The words of their friend struck me as if they were a shock. My walls weren't barriers that shielded me; they were just walls that kept others from entering. As time passed, I began accepting those awkward moments when I was vulnerable and exposed. I stopped believing that others tried to alter me and started to think they offered me their piece--one I could develop by letting the piece into.

It's a phrase I hold to now: *"Growth doesn't happen in comfort."* The tense of opposing perspectives was more about right and proper and more about learning how to weave the threads of knowledge to build something greater than me. These experiences gave me patience whenever I felt like snapping and lashing out, empathy when I wanted to move on the other side, and humility even when my self-confidence urged me to do the opposite.

When I chose to pay attention and look around, I found new nooks of mine. Disparities stopped being a hindrance. They became bridges that brought together not only our thoughts but also our hearts. For that, I am forever thankful.

Narrating Perspectives: Compatibility In Harmonious Coexistence

The Dinner Recipe Debate

Me: "I think this pasta will taste better with cream. It's how my mom always made it."

Spouse: "That does sound good, but what if we tried olive oil and garlic instead? It's lighter and brings out the flavors of the veggies."

Me: "But cream is so comforting... Olive oil feels too simple."

Spouse: "I get that, but let's try my way this time. If it doesn't work, we'll do it your way next time."

Me: (Pausing, realizing the collaboration) "Okay, let's do it. Maybe we'll find a new favorite together."

The Vacation Dilemma

Me: "I think a beach vacation would be perfect. Just us, the sun, and the waves. No stress."

Spouse: "That does sound relaxing, but what about the mountains? I've been wanting to hike and explore a bit more."

Me: "We're going for peace, not a workout!"

Spouse: (Laughing) "I hear you, but isn't finding peace also about reconnecting with nature? Maybe we can find a mountain cabin with a view?"

Me: "You know, that could work. A little mix of both. Let's look into it."

The Parenting Puzzle

Me: "I think we need to set stricter rules about bedtime. They're staying up way too late."

Spouse: "I see your point, but maybe they're staying up because they don't get enough one-on-one time with us."

Me: "So you're saying it's our fault?"

Spouse: "Not at all. Just wondering if tweaking our evening routine could help them settle down easier."

Me: (Reflecting) "Hmm. That's worth trying. Let's dedicate a little time before bed just for them and see how it goes."

The Home Renovation Standoff

Me: "I really think we should paint the walls white. It's timeless and brightens up the space."

Spouse: "White is nice, but it feels a bit sterile. A soft blue could bring in some warmth."

Me: "Sterile? It's called minimalism!"

Spouse: "And I love your minimalist style. Let's pick a shade that's light but has a touch of personality."

Me: (Smiling) "Alright, soft blue it is. You always find a way to blend our ideas."

The Career Advice Clash

Me: "I'm thinking of taking that new job offer. It pays more, and I can't pass that up."

Spouse: "I get it, but have you thought about the longer commute? You've been valuing your free time a lot lately."

Me: "True, but more money means more security for us. Isn't that important?"

Spouse: "Absolutely. Just want you to be sure it's worth sacrificing your downtime. Let's weigh the pros and cons together."

Me: "Good idea. I might have been too focused on the money part. Thanks for grounding me."

The Beauty in Diversity

Diversity is the essence of our existence; it adds colour to our lives and deepens our relationships. In family, romantic, or platonic relationships, the differences in perspective, background, and perspectives can contribute to a greater understanding of ourselves and those around us. Recognizing and appreciating our differences can unlock new perspectives and insights that otherwise go unexplored.

Personalized Relationship Dynamics

It was once a time when I believed that harmony came out of similarities. Fewer differences mean fewer clashes; wasn't that the recipe to peace? But my experience taught me that it wasn't. It revealed that diversity, which was something to be navigating, was the way towards a deeper understanding and reflection of the things I didn't recognize.

Being around someone so distinct from me was my first experience. I've always enjoyed spontaneousness and enjoying being unprepared. My spouse was on the other side, seeking comfort in the routine and structure. Initially, his desire to be in control felt overwhelming, as if walls were closing in over my liberty. However, then something changed. I realized that his daily routine created a sense of calm in my chaotic life. It was not confined; it was grounding. My impulsiveness started to lead him into times of surprise joy. We both learned to let go of our grip on what we believed was "right."

It's not just about the personalities. I recall a conversation with people whose culture was quite different from my own, and the person initially seemed a bit alien. His quiet respect for elders and deep dedication to tradition made me smile. I started to view humility from a fresh perspective and carry that into my interactions. He was the one in which I noticed a spark of curiosity that prompted me to consider how his life could look if he were to stray away from the carefully drawn lines.

The most challenging challenging part of the diversity issue lies in navigating ideological divisions. In one instance, I was arguing with him over the values we believed in. The conflict was difficult to resolve as if our bond would break because of our polarities. However, we encountered some common threads over time and through slow talks. *"We can disagree and still love each other,"* I remember saying to him. It was true since what binds us is more significant than the things that separate us.

The most important insight was this: Diversity isn't an obstacle. It's a chance to be welcomed. Every difference opens a way to enter, and we learn with each step we step through the door. Sometimes, we feel uncomfortable--when viewpoints clash or our beliefs conflict--we're extended beyond the limits of what we believe could become.

That area is where natural natural beauty is found, in the shades we did not know existed and only recognized through contrast. *The world's diversity doesn't simply make us uncomfortable; it also completes our lives.*

Narrating Perspectives: Compatibility In Diversity

The Spontaneous Weekend Trip vs. the Planned Routine

Me: "Let's pack a bag and just go somewhere this weekend. No plans, no schedules, just the open road and us."

My Spouse: *smiling gently* "That sounds fun, but let's at least book a place to stay. I know you love surprises, but I feel more comfortable knowing where we'll sleep."

Me: *sighing playfully* "Fine. But no itinerary once we get there, okay?"

My Spouse: "Deal. You bring the adventure; I'll make sure we're not stranded. It's a perfect balance."

Cultural Curiosity at Dinner

Me: "You always bow slightly when serving your parents food. It's so respectful. Is it a tradition in your family?"

My Spouse: "Yes, it's a way of showing gratitude. I noticed you always start conversations at the table with a question; that seems to bring everyone closer together."

Me: "I suppose it does. Maybe we're both trying to connect, just in our own ways."

My Spouse: *nodding* "It's interesting how different habits reflect the same intentions."

Clashing Over Ideals

Me: "I can't believe you'd see it that way. It feels like you're defending something I deeply disagree with."

My Spouse: "I'm not defending it; I'm trying to understand it from another perspective. Maybe we're missing some common ground."

Me: *pausing* "Okay, let's start there. Why is this important to you?"

My Spouse: "Because it challenges me to think beyond my comfort zone. I think we both care about the same things, but our approaches differ."

Me: "Maybe you're right. Let's figure it out together."

Parenting Styles: Freedom vs. Structure

Me: "Let them stay up late tonight; it's just one night! It's about making memories."

My Spouse: *firmly* "But they need a routine, even on weekends. It's better for them long-term."

Me: *after a moment* "What if we let them stay up but keep the bedtime story routine? A bit of both worlds?"

My Spouse: *smiling* "I think that could work. They get their fun, and we don't disrupt their rhythm too much."

Worldview Conversations on a Starry Night

Me: "Sometimes I think life is about enjoying the present, not worrying so much about the future."

My Spouse: "I see what you mean, but planning gives me peace of mind. It feels like I'm protecting what we have."

Me: *gazing at the stars* "Maybe your plans are the anchor, and my spontaneity is the wind. Together, we make the perfect ship."

My Spouse: *laughing* "That's beautiful. As long as we're sailing together, I'm happy."

Personal Growth Through Acceptance

If we accept the differences of others by opening our hearts and minds, we set off in a process of personal development. Accepting another's perspective forces the mind to examine our beliefs and preconceptions. Reflection on our own beliefs and assumptions allows us to grow beyond the comfort zone of our lives. When we encounter different opinions, it prompts reflection regarding our beliefs and values. The ability to understand different viewpoints increases the ability of us to understand other people's experiences. Being able to adapt to the new paradigm increases mental agility as well as problem-solving capabilities.

Personalized Relationship Dynamics

I once believed I was in control of my life--like my beliefs were written in the stone of time, unchangeable and indestructible. The truths I believed in were as strong as protection from any challenge to them. But the world can humble even the most steadfast within us. In my case, it came through one conversation I could not keep from having with an individual whose views were opposite to mine.

My initial reaction was to fight from clinging to the things I "knew" to be true. I took a stand against curiosity instead of confrontation for reasons not entirely clear. "Why do you see it that way?" I attempted to dispel the anger bubbling inside me. When they began to speak, I experienced something awe-inspiring--a gap in the belief system I'd held so tightly. The feeling wasn't pleasant; asking questions about the truth of your convictions is never comfortable. It was as if you were pulling on an untied thread of an intricately woven tapestry, uncertain whether the whole tapestry would break.

However, amid that apprehension, I discovered the possibility of growth. I reaffirmed myself: "Acceptance doesn't mean agreement." This doesn't mean that I have to give up the person I am or what I believe in. It's more about creating room in my heart to accept opinions that aren't my own. When I did this, I wasn't lost. I discovered new layers, empathy I never thought I could have, and honesty, which has made my life richer and fuller.

I realized the meaning of listening to someone not only with my ears but also with my heart. Listening to someone's story in the way they told it and not just through the lens of my own experiences. A few days ago, following an extremely deep discussion, I thought, *"What if I walked in their shoes?"* Then, as I imagined their experience, I could see glimpses of my humanness reflected in me. It was very humbling and even somewhat unsettling. But it was also liberating.

As I've discovered, the growth path is not about transforming others but about changing ourselves. It's about giving up the desire to guard our boundaries and opening doors for others to come into. If we let others in it, we do not become less who we were; our identity is enlarged. It's not a surrender but an invitation to move with the tempo of life, with grace and acceptance. Through this, I've come to a more profound and complete self-image that does not fear difference anymore but accepts it.

Narrating Perspectives: Compatibility In Personal Growth Through Acceptance

Understanding Family Traditions

Spouse: "You know, I've always wondered why you're so insistent on celebrating that holiday every year. It's not something my family ever did, and honestly, it feels like a lot of work for no reason."

Me: "I get that. It's just something I grew up with. For me, it's about remembering where I come from and keeping those connections alive."

Spouse: "I never thought of it that way. I guess I've always seen holidays as optional or even stressful. But if it's important to you, maybe I can try seeing it through your eyes."

Me: "Thanks for saying that. I don't expect you to love it immediately, but your openness means a lot."

Spouse: "And who knows? Maybe I'll find something meaningful in it for myself."

Differing Approaches to Problem-Solving

Me: "I can't believe you just told your friend you'd help them move next weekend. We already had plans!"

Spouse: "I know, but they really need help, and I couldn't say no. They've been there for me before."

Me: "I guess I just value sticking to commitments over being there for people last minute. But I see your point; loyalty is important to you."

Spouse: "It's just how I've always been. But I can see how it might feel like I'm prioritizing others over us sometimes."

Me: "Maybe it's not about right or wrong. It's about understanding why we make these choices. Let's figure out a way to balance it better."

Spouse: "I'd like that. I want to be there for both you and the people I care about."

Political Differences

Spouse: "You always seem so skeptical about my views on this issue. Do you think I'm wrong?"
Me: "Not wrong, just…different. Your perspective challenges mine, and I've realized that's not a bad thing."
Spouse: "That's surprising to hear. I assumed you thought I was just stubborn."
Me: "No, it's more that I'm used to thinking one way, and hearing your views forces me to step out of that. It's uncomfortable but important."
Spouse: "I feel the same when you bring up your ideas. I don't always agree, but I respect the thought behind them."
Me: "Maybe that's the point: learning from each other instead of trying to change each other."

Parenting Styles

Me: "You're always so laid-back when the kids are upset. Don't you think they need more discipline?"
Spouse: "I do, but I also think they need someone to listen first. My parents were strict, and it made me feel like my feelings didn't matter."
Me: "That's interesting. My parents were the opposite, and sometimes I felt lost without clear guidance."
Spouse: "So maybe we balance each other out? You bring the structure, and I bring the empathy."
Me: "I like that idea. Instead of clashing, we can work together to give them the best of both worlds."

Cultural Identity

Spouse: "I've noticed you've been teaching the kids about your language and traditions, but not mine. Why is that?"

Me: "I guess I assumed they'd pick up yours naturally since we live here. But maybe I've overlooked how important it is to you."

Spouse: "It is. I want them to feel connected to both sides of their heritage."

Me: "You're right. Let's find ways to teach them about both. Maybe we can do something together, like cooking dishes from your culture or celebrating both our holidays."

Spouse: "That sounds perfect. It's not about one or the other—it's about creating something that reflects all of who they are."

Finding Middle Ground

The intricate relationship between dance and finding common ground for everyone is simultaneously an art and science. When we traverse the many environments of our relationships and relationships, it is crucial to devise strategies that enable our bodies to adjust and flourish in the face of different perspectives.

Personalized Relationship Dynamics

Finding the middle is an extremely transformational element of our marriage. The goal wasn't to reach a consensus on everything but to be able to adapt and grow together.

We take our morning routines, For instance. One of us is a fan of routines and starts daily with a task agenda and plan. Another prefers the flexibility of a leisurely, unstructured beginning. Initially, these two views were a bit tense but loud. However, instead of going on with the fight, we tried experimenting. We would have weekends where we put together a laid-back arrangement and set aside a few hours to work on shared objectives, including meal prep or organization. When we listened to each other's wants, we turned any friction into a bond.

Planning a trip to the airport was a different, enjoyable learning experience. We both love planning meticulously planned itineraries, while another enjoys the excitement of exploring on your own. In the beginning, holidays felt like a battleground of different preferences. Over time, however, we adapted to a system of alternate approaches. The day could be scheduled, and then we would go to the cafe for lunch. What about the next day? Spontaneous. *"You don't always have to meet halfway,"* we were reminded, repeating the advice we cherish, "but be willing to move." This attitude was a source of joy and uncertainty in our journeys.

The ability to adapt extends to communicating. When we have disagreements, it is important to not aim at winning instead of focusing on the sake of understanding. For example, phrases such as "I see your point" or "Help me understand why this matters to you" were our way of communicating. The goal wasn't to erase the differences in our views but to make room for our fellows.

What we've discovered is the fact that adapting doesn't mean loss of ourselves. The process is expanding and evolving into an ever-more compassionate and multifaceted persona of what we are. This can be done through simple actions such as rotating the choice of a Friday night film or more profound changes like reviewing longer-term goals; and finding a middle to help find a common purpose.

The great thing about this method is that it's never flawless, and yet it's worthwhile. The most effective bonds aren't built upon the sameness of but rather an intention to improve.

Narrating Perspectives: Compatibility In Finding Middle Ground

The Morning Routine Conflict

Me: "I know you thrive with a solid plan for the day, but I feel stressed when everything is structured. What if we try a hybrid approach?"
Spouse: "A hybrid approach? What do you have in mind?"
Me: "Maybe on weekdays, we stick to a plan for productivity, and on weekends, we can have relaxed mornings without any agendas."
Spouse: "That sounds fair. Let's try it for a month and see how it feels."

The Travel Style Compromise

Spouse: "I love exploring on the fly without a strict plan, but I see you feel more comfortable when things are organized. How do we make this work?"
Me: "How about this: we plan one major activity each day, like visiting a landmark, but leave afternoons free for spontaneous exploring?"
Spouse: "I love that balance. It gives me the thrill of the unexpected while still making you feel secure."
Me: "Great! And we can tweak it as we go if needed."

The Friday Movie Night Debate

Me: "I know you're not into sci-fi, but I was really hoping to watch this space exploration film tonight."
Spouse: "Hmm, I was leaning towards a comedy. Can we take turns choosing the movie?"
Me: "That works! We can watch the comedy next Friday, and for

tonight, how about some popcorn to sweeten the deal?"
Spouse: "Deal! And I'll pick the comedy next week."

Planning Household Chores

Spouse: "I feel overwhelmed when the chores pile up. Can we divide them more evenly?"
Me: "I get that. I tend to tackle them in bursts, but I see how it's not working for you. What's a good way to split it?"
Spouse: "Maybe we list all tasks and pick the ones we don't mind doing. We can alternate weekly for the rest."
Me: "I like that. Let's give it a try and adjust if it's not working."

Dinner Preferences Clash

Spouse: "I was hoping for takeout tonight, but I know you prefer cooking at home."
Me: "What if we cook together? Maybe a simple dish that's quick, and we save takeout for another day when we're both too tired?"
Spouse: "Cooking together sounds nice. And takeout can be our treat for the weekend!"
Me: "Perfect! Let's make pasta tonight—it's fast and easy."

The Art of Compromise

It is usually viewed as a way to compromise, but it's an effective tool to build bridges across divergent routes. By understanding each other's needs and wants, couples can find solutions that respect each other's views.

Personalized Relationship Dynamics

In one instance, it was an unforgiving idea for me. It was as if I would compromise a portion of myself to find tranquillity. Then, I realized that it was not the time to compromise. It was all about finding the right rhythm and balance to make two voices sing.

I was sitting in the middle of the road when two thoughts flew in opposite directions. One aimed at the bustling cities brimming with possibilities and lights, and the other aimed to have a more tranquil life focusing on home and the simple things in life. Both of us seemed incompatible, unrelated. Discussions were stressful and filled with *"But this is what I want"* and *"You just don't understand."* Conversations were circular; I felt they were frustrated and in a different world, and things were frustrating. Instead of trying to defend our desires, we asked each other, *"What would staying here take away from you?"* and *"What scares you most about leaving?"* The answers revealed fears that had never been thought about. The city might mean the desired job, but it also signifies the relationship of loved ones. The fact that you were there indicated being in a group and the chance of failing to achieve the goals you set. Then, we stopped seeing each other as obstacles and began to see ourselves as partners for each other.

Also, we've learned that compromises can be based on something other than large decision-making. It's more about everyday decisions:

- Which person takes care of the chores when everyone is exhausted?

- How they can spend their spare time.

- What to cook to be served for dinner when the cravings aren't in sync.

The goal isn't about accumulating victories but recognizing each other's needs. We both love holidays at the beach, while one loves urban landscapes. We, therefore, split our time in the ocean with a serene morning and bustling urban excursions. We both leave happy and not reluctantly settling for.

When those moments were candid, there was a clear indication that there had been a middle road. It was not far from home yet close to a career path. The two of us did not attain what we had hoped for. The feeling was that it wasn't as if we lost. It was like we had created our own innovative thing.

Compromise: I've learned that the most victories don't need to be about being successful but rather understanding. It's about letting go of the notion that a single route is the best way and finding a way that is a tribute to the heart of each. There was no solution to a challenge; however, we came to know the other person more strongly than before. We've realized that *"Compromise is the art of allowing love to lead over pride."* Every compromise we make reinforces our bond and helps us remember why we chose this particular path.

With compromise, we're more than only negotiating a compromise; we're creating a new life that is truly and uniquely ours. We've discovered that this to be the most satisfying victory of all.

Narrating Perspectives: Compatibility In Finding Middle Ground

The Kitchen Chore Debate

Me: "I've had such a long day. Can you handle the dishes tonight?"
Spouse: "I'm just as exhausted as you. Can we skip doing them until tomorrow?"
Me: "I hate waking up to a messy kitchen. What if I do the dishes now, and you take care of breakfast in the morning?"
Spouse: "That works. I'll make sure breakfast is ready before you wake up."

Vacation Dilemma

Spouse: "I want to go hiking in the mountains for our trip this year. The fresh air and nature will be so refreshing."
Me: "But I've been dreaming about lounging by the beach, reading under the sun."
Spouse: "What if we spend three days in the mountains, and then head to the coast for a few more days?"
Me: "Perfect. That way, we both get the break we need."

Dinner Dispute

Me: "I'm craving Italian tonight. A big plate of lasagna sounds perfect."
Spouse: "Italian again? I was thinking sushi. Something light for dinner."
Me: "How about we order Italian tonight and sushi this

weekend? Or maybe even get both tonight and share?"

Spouse: "Let's share! I'd love to try a bit of lasagna with my sushi."

Weekend Plans

Spouse: "I want to spend Saturday catching up on work. I'm really behind."

Me: "But we haven't had a date night in ages. I was hoping for a nice dinner out."

Spouse: "How about I work until 5 PM, then we head out for an early dinner? That way, I'll get some work done, and we'll still have our evening together."

Me: "That sounds fair. I'll plan for a reservation at 6."

Big Move Decision

Me: "I really want to move closer to my family. I miss them so much."

Spouse: "But my job is here, and it's such a great opportunity. I don't want to start over elsewhere."

Me: "What if we moved halfway between both places? You could still commute to your job, and we'd be closer to my family."

Spouse: "That's worth considering. Let's research areas and see how it could work."

The Key to Understanding

The act of listening extends beyond just listening to words. It involves completely engaging your friend's thoughts and feelings. This method builds compassion and can help uncover the deeper issues that might not immediately be apparent.

Personalized Relationship Dynamics

My partner and I began noticing an underlying pattern of miscommunication; we felt like we were in a marathon, putting our bodies through the air and getting nowhere. Discussions on chores, scheduling, and even small things like what to do with the dishwasher would happen repeatedly. It wasn't until the time we stopped to *hear* one another that things started to change.

A few nights ago, in an argument, we decided to take a break to try something new. Instead of being rushed to reply or argue, we simply took a deep breath and listened. I was listening. It was not easy. Sometimes, one is tempted to come up with a solution, a reason. However, something extraordinary occurred by remaining silent and giving one another the space to breathe.

For example, I have stated, *"I feel like you don't notice the effort I put into keeping things organized."* This wasn't only about the mess; it was about acknowledging. In addition, since my partner did not challenge or interrupt my thoughts, I felt secure enough to explore further. This space of vulnerability was an enormous difference.

My partner told me a few times, *"When I come home, I need ten minutes to unwind before diving into conversations or tasks."* Before, I could have interpreted this to mean a lack of interest or defiance; however, clarifying the whole thing helped me see that the issue wasn't really about me. It was all about recharge.

Through active listening, we learned that listening isn't just about resolving problems but accepting the feelings behind them. It's about saying I'm with your voice. We're here to help. It's been learned to ask clarifying questions like *"What do you need from me right now--support or solutions?"* Small changes like these boost connections and build a stronger bond.

It's not a magic solution to all disputes; it is a potent instrument for building mutual compassion and understanding. As my partner put the idea beautifully, *"It's the quiet that helps us hear each other's hearts."*

Narrating Perspectives: Compatibility In Understanding

The Dishwasher Dilemma

Me: "I feel frustrated when the dishwasher is left half-empty after dinner. It feels like I'm doing double work."
Spouse: *[Pauses for a moment]* "I hear you. It's not that I don't want to help; sometimes, I'm just so drained after the day. I guess I need a system that feels doable at the moment."
Me: "Thank you for sharing. What if we agree to alternate evenings, so neither of us feels overwhelmed?"
Spouse: "That sounds fair. Let's give it a try."

The Weekend Plan Puzzle

Me: "I was really looking forward to spending Saturday together, but I feel like your plans with friends might be taking that away."
Spouse: "I didn't realize you felt that way. Saturday wasn't meant to replace our time; I just thought you might enjoy some

downtime while I caught up with them."

Me: "That's fair. Maybe we could do breakfast together before your plans? That way, I still get time with you."

Spouse: "That's a great idea. Breakfast it is!"

The Laundry Load

Me: "I noticed the laundry hasn't been folded, and it's piling up. It feels like it's all on me."

Spouse: "I'm sorry you're feeling overwhelmed. I've been caught up in other things and didn't realize how much it was bothering you."

Me: "It's okay. Can we work together on it tomorrow? Maybe make it a shared task while we watch a movie?"

Spouse: "I'd like that. Let's do it."

The Evening Quiet Request

Me: "When you come home and go straight to your room without talking, I feel like you're avoiding me."

Spouse: "I see how that might feel hurtful. It's not that I'm avoiding you. I just need a few minutes to unwind after work before I can be fully present."

Me: "I didn't know that. Thank you for telling me. What if I give you space when you get home, and we catch up after dinner?"

Spouse: "That's perfect. I really appreciate you understanding."

The Acknowledgment Moment

Me: "Sometimes, I feel like my efforts around the house go unnoticed. I'm not looking for praise, but a simple thank you would mean a lot."

Spouse: "I didn't realize you felt that way. I truly appreciate everything you do; I guess I've been bad at showing it."

Me: "That acknowledgment right there means so much. Let's try

to make appreciation a regular thing for both of us."
Spouse: "I love that idea. Let's make it happen."

Cultivating Flexibility

The ability to adapt is essential to the unpredictable nature of life. Being flexible and open-minded lets couples move effortlessly when confronted with unexpected difficulties. Because they are open to change and learn from each other's traditions and traditions, they strengthen their bonds through new knowledge and experiences.

Personalized Relationship Dynamics

It was the time that we believed that love alone was the only way to achieve peace and that shared goals and laughter could bridge all gaps. But life taught us a humbling truth: *love needs a steadfast partner--flexibility*. Through our triumphs and trials and triumphs, we realized that cultivating flexibility didn't mean being a loser but rather creating an existence that was respectful of each of our lives.

It was a meal we shared with family members, and we imagined it would be a simple combination of warmth and laughter. But the actual event was far more complicated. My family was awed by the spontaneity of life, and my spouse loved rituals. A simple thing as simple as the seating arrangement became a source that caused friction. We initially saw the issue as challenging but considered, *"How can we honor what matters to them? "* This change revealed that these particulars aren't merely trivial. They carry importance, significance, and a sense of the culture. We accepted compromise and learned to blend the spontaneity of one family's life and the customs of another. What did we get? An even richer web of connections.

The flexibility of our lives was evident in our exploration of our own goals for our lives. One was a fan of busy city life with vibrant communities; another longed to spend quiet days in the countryside. They were not just desires but reflections of the innermost parts of us. Instead of letting it cause us to be divided, we changed how we looked at our thoughts: *What if we could merge the best aspects of two sides?* Together, we discovered a common dream: a peaceful place to live in despite the bustle of the city. This gave us the peace we wanted.

There followed the daily lessons. For instance, controlling time: one person is drawn to structure, and the other prefers a more flexible approach. In creating "flexible routines," we found ourselves in the middle. We planned; however, we would allow ourselves to be spontaneous, such as penciling during the evening, but let the events unfold naturally. We often recall, *"Flexibility is the art of bending without breaking."*

Every negotiation, every bit of compromise, has shown that flexibility doesn't weaken affection but may enhance it. Understanding the individuality of each member when forming goals together is not just an emotion; it's an important factor that grows with time, evolves, and blossoms.

Narrating Perspectives: Compatibility In Flexibility

The Dinner Seating Plan

Me: "I noticed you're particular about where everyone sits during dinner. Why is that important to you?"
Spouse: "It's a tradition in my family; it helps everyone feel included and connected."

Me: "That's interesting. In my family, we just sit wherever feels right in the moment. What if we tried assigning seats for special dinners and kept it casual for regular meals?"
Spouse: "I like that idea. It respects both approaches!"

City or Countryside Dreams

Spouse: "I love the energy of the city—there's always something happening."
Me: "And I crave the peace and quiet of open spaces. The noise of the city sometimes feels overwhelming."
Spouse: "What if we found a place just outside the city? Close enough for its vibrancy but peaceful enough to feel like a retreat?"
Me: "That sounds perfect. We'd get the best of both worlds."

The Spontaneous Weekend

Me: "I was thinking we could plan out the whole weekend. You know, activities, timings, everything."
Spouse: "I'd rather keep it open. Plans can sometimes feel restrictive."
Me: "What if we listed a few key things we'd love to do and left the timing flexible?"
Spouse: "That could work. It gives us some direction but keeps the freedom to enjoy the moment."

Handling Family Traditions

Spouse: "Your family is so spontaneous during gatherings. It's fun but a little chaotic for me."
Me: "And your family is so structured—it's beautiful but sometimes feels too rigid."
Spouse: "What if we introduced a balance? We could set a loose structure but let people decide how to engage within it."
Me: "I love that. It could make everyone feel at ease."

Balancing Time Management Styles

Me: "You always want to have everything planned out, and I admire that, but sometimes I feel like it's too much."
Spouse: "And I admire your spontaneity, but I sometimes feel it's disorganized."
Me: "What if we created a 'flexible schedule'? For example, we'd plan our mornings but leave afternoons open for whatever comes up."
Spouse: "I like that—it gives structure but also room for spontaneity."

Setting Boundaries Together

Setting boundaries is essential to creating individual identities in a group. When done with a team, establishing boundaries improves respect for each other and trust. Defining together, the non-negotiables for everyone involved, like dedicated evenings with the family -- created a structure that facilitated personal development and harmony between relationships.

Personalized Relationship Dynamics

It was challenging to know just what boundaries meant for us. It seemed at first as if it was enough. If we truly cared, we would naturally comprehend and appreciate each other's requirements. As time passed, it became clear that love doesn't have to be just cutting the dividing lines between two individuals. The goal is to draw them out with attention, not so they can be separated but to create a space we can both be part of but not be lost.

One of the things we noticed was that the work schedule began to creep into our lives. The evenings we had planned to have with each other turned into endless checking emails as weekends became an extension of our work week. Then, one evening, following a quiet dinner, I asked, *"What's one thing you need to feel connected again?"* This question was an important crucial turning point.

We started small. No phones during meals. This may sound simple; however, the impact was significant. Without screens that could sway our attention, the dinner table became a space for us to reconnect. We'd talk about funny times we had shared, discuss our hopes and dreams, and relax in a quiet space. We were reminded of why we enjoyed being in our friendship.

We then made an order: No working after 9 pm. Initially, it was difficult to close the laptops and ignore the phone sound. However, we realized that the world would not stop for us, and time with each other was now sacred. We'd play board games together, take a trip to the movies, or walk through the streets, hands in hand, under the starry skies.

We were also aware of the value of having our own space. Every Sunday, we set time alone to journal, read, or do other activities. This wasn't only refreshing; it allowed us to return to one another with a new enthusiasm. *"Me time isn't selfish,"* we remarked. *"It's a gift we give to us both."*

Each boundary was not a limitation but rather an act of respect. Every person was able to say, *"I see you. I love you. I value us."* Even though it required patience, those lines became the pillars of a lifestyle where loved ones could thrive.

Narrating Perspectives: Compatibility In Setting Boundaries

Discussing Work-Life Balance

Over dinner, phones tucked away in the other room:

Me: "I've been thinking about how often work spills over into our evenings. It feels like we're losing our time together."

Spouse: "I've noticed that too. I hate that we're sitting next to each other but barely connecting."

Me: "What if we set a rule—no work after 9 pm? We could use that time to relax and really be present."

Spouse: "That's a great idea. Let's try it for a week and see how it feels."

Prioritizing Quality Time

While walking in the park:

Me: "I miss the little things we used to do, like movie nights or just laughing over board games."

Spouse: "I do too. It's like everything else has taken over. How do you think we can bring that back?"

Me: "Maybe we dedicate one evening a week to just us—no phones, no distractions."

Spouse: "I'd love that. Let's make it official. Friday nights are now ours."

Establishing Personal Space

On a quiet Sunday morning:

Spouse: "I've been feeling a little overwhelmed lately. It's not about you—I think I just need some time to recharge."

Me: "I get that. I feel the same way sometimes. How about we set aside time every Sunday for ourselves? You can do your thing, and I'll do mine."

Spouse: "That sounds perfect. It's like giving each other room to grow but staying connected."

Me: "Exactly. Then we can share what we've been up to afterward."

Communicating Boundaries During Stressful Times

Late at night after a long day:

Me: "I noticed you've been really quiet this week. Is everything okay?"

Spouse: "It's just work. I don't want to dump it all on you."

Me: "You don't have to handle it alone, but maybe we can set some limits. Like, no work emails after a certain time?"

Spouse: "That might help. And maybe I can talk to you about it earlier in the evening so it doesn't build up."

Me: "Of course. We're a team—we'll figure it out together."

Navigating Social Commitments

During a weekend planning session:

Spouse: "We've been saying yes to so many things lately. I feel like we barely have time to breathe."

Me: "I feel the same. Maybe we need to set a boundary with social events—like no more than one commitment per weekend."

Spouse: "That's a great idea. It'll give us time to actually relax and focus on us."

Me: "Exactly. Plus, we'll be able to enjoy the plans we do make instead of feeling stretched thin."

The Role of Patience in Adaptation

Patience is often underestimated but plays an integral role in adaptation strategies. Building compatibility takes time; rushing the process can lead to frustration or resentment.

Personalized Relationship Dynamics

The first time we met when we first met, we had a mixture of different personalities. One of us is a fan of spontaneousness and enjoys the excitement of having plans at the last minute, whereas another prefers order and prefers things laid out. In those early days, our differences clashed like cymbals, and even the most minor decisions felt like negotiations--choosing a dinner spot could stretch into a half-hour of back-and-forth.

Patience became our quiet guide. It wasn't something that we were actively looking for, but we came across that it was necessary. It whispered, *"Pause, listen, and try to see through their eyes."* Instead of being adamant about our old ways of thinking, we started to change. The planner enjoyed the joy at unexpected moments, like the unplanned deviation from an excursion that brought us to the finest coffee spot we've visited. The spontaneous one began to discover the beauty of thoughtful planning, for example, planning a surprise picnic that includes everything necessary to have a great day.

We learned that patience isn't about letting other people's quirks go but instead celebrating these quirks. The moments that were once a mystery to us, like someone who rearranged their books in colour or checked twice an unpacked suitcase, became charming. Then we realized that these routines were not just inconveniences but a reflection of who we indeed are.

We often refer to each other: *"Patience does not refer to waiting around, but the capacity to maintain an attitude of calm while waiting."* We lived this reality every time we had to work out a solution or reach a compromise about something significant, such as where we should be living. Through listening, truly listening, we could understand each other's fears and hopes.

Boundaries were a staple of our perseverance. They weren't barriers but bridges that helped us understand our needs meaningfully. When we needed time to ourselves after a long day, our others agreed, knowing that recognizing those needs benefited us all.

Our rhythm has become that of a common one. It's been our experience that harmony isn't just about the sameness of people but instead being able to understand and grow together. *With patience, we realized that differences don't constitute obstacles but rather the foundation for an intimate relationship filled with balance, love, and flexibility.* We laughed and were reminded to compromise, even on the smallest of things.

Narrating Perspectives: Compatibility In Patience in Adaptation

The Last-Minute Dinner Debate

Me: "How about we try that new Italian place tonight? I saw some great reviews!"

Spouse: "I'd prefer to decide earlier; it's already 7 PM, and I'm not sure we'll get a table."

Me: "You're right. How about I call ahead and check if they can accommodate us?"

Spouse: "That works. I appreciate you taking a moment to think about my schedule."

The Forgotten Grocery List

Spouse: "Did you remember the shopping list? I made sure it was ready this morning."

Me: "I got everything I thought we needed… but I might have missed a few things."

Spouse: "Let's go through what we have. I can help you double-check next time."

Me: "That would be great. I'm still getting used to your organized style."

The Perfect Holiday Plan

Spouse: "I planned out our whole trip itinerary! Check this out."

Me: "This is really detailed. Can we leave some time for wandering around, though?"

Spouse: "Absolutely. Let's slot in a few hours each day for free exploration."

Me: "Perfect! I love that we're making room for both our styles."

The Quiet Evening

Me: "It's been a long day. I just want to sit in silence for a bit."

Spouse: "Of course. Do you want some tea while you relax?"

Me: "Thanks. Afterward, I'd love to hear about your day."

Spouse: "Take your time. We'll talk when you're ready."

The Rearranged Bookshelf

Me: "Did you change the bookshelf order again?"

Spouse: "I did! It's by genre now—it makes finding things so much easier."

Me: "It looks great. I'll make a note so I don't disrupt your system."

Spouse: "Thank you! I love that you're trying to adapt."

Professional Paradox

Like a river in motion, life demands that its currents are balanced. Ambition is like a strong stream that propels you forward. It shapes your dreams and carves paths. Alongside this fierce pursuit, a more subtle current flows--the constant pull of intimacy and affection. The two currents often cross, but where they do, there is a turbulent water that forces us to be careful so we don't get swept up by either one.

Imagine the warmth of the sun rising in the morning, calling us awake to embrace the day and pursue the horizon. As night begins to fall, the constant moonlight comforts us, reminding us of our home and the places we left behind as we pursue that ever-elusive, elusive horizon. The tension that exists between professional ambitions and personal obligations is reflected in this interplay. This dynamic has been around as long as the human race itself. We often forget the relationships we have built over time as we strive to be more and reach higher. These connections can become more fragile as we progress.

Time becomes an elusive concept in the frenzy of a career. It slips through our hands like sand. We are on a business trip in a busy city where streets vibrate with possibilities. The conversations flow as wine, and the connections ignite. For a brief moment, this seems to be all that exists. In the silence of our hotel room, after the chaos has subsided, we remember what we have left behind. Perhaps a partner is sitting alone at the table in your kitchen with two plates and utensils. Irony aside, success, the prize that we all strive for, is often the brightest when it's not shared with those who matter most.

Our resilience and optimism are a part of our nature. Our rivers flow harmoniously because we find a way to get over these challenges. The forest is reminded of its interconnectedness by the whispering wind in the trees. We can reaffirm our bonds with small acts of kindness, such as a simple phone call or letter.

It is the delicate dance between ambition and love that makes us reflect on our choices. The dance asks that we find calm in the midst of storms and cherish our roots while chasing what motivates us. The union of multiple streams forms the most substantial rivers. Each stream is vital for the overall journey.

Opportunities for Connection Beyond Professional Boundaries

By its very nature, the work environment is an interaction with others. Every day, we are in situations in which we are interacting with people within situations that are often highly challenging and sometimes even celebratory. In these situations, there is a tendency to see the lines between the professional and personal disappear. When we interact with people, we have in common the mission of our business and the same day, night, worries, and days. They become friends who share in-depth jokes, miscommunications, and sometimes even private confidences. That is what makes up the "professional paradox"- an environment built for efficiency that, often by design, creates an entirely different and, at times, personal.

Realities of Professional Life

At one point, I thought that work and my personal life were two distinct realms, each with its routines and rules. Over time, I've realized how easily these boundaries can be blurred. Something unexpected occurs within the shared space of offices or in the intimateness of late-night Zoom calls. Conversations that were once only professional become personal. Some people whom you considered colleagues are now acquaintances, perhaps even family. At these times, work becomes more complicated.

I've witnessed this happen personally during times of high-stakes deadlines. The sound of computers late into the night, laughter working through tension, and the camaraderie of fatigue create a bond unlike none other. The demands to achieve goals erode our usual barriers, revealing our human nature. Someone once said,

"You don't know your coworkers until you've pulled an all-nighter together." They had a point. At these times, there is a rift between personal and professional, which is virtually non-existent.

The same relationships that bring joy can cause problems, particularly when feelings blur the lines. It's been my experience how simple it can be to allow a sense of camaraderie to transform into something more significant, for admiration to transform into affection, or for conversations between friends to drift into risky territory. The initial impression is subtle; it's almost invisible. An exchange of jokes is transformed into a long-lasting gaze. An ordinary coffee shop visit becomes something to be awaited or even desired. Ultimately, the boundaries between personal and professional life have become blurred.

This situation is made more tense in the event of power imbalances. Once, I observed one of my team members confiding with their boss concerning personal challenges, finding confidence in their direction. This initial support exchange became more intimate and unbalanced, a bond hidden in confusion and secrecy. Trust that was the initial factor in bringing the two together later was a cause of hurt. The professional relationships began to unravel, and the group's trust and confidence deteriorated, causing ripples that affected all.

The problem is more comprehensive than offices. Travel for business, in addition, may accelerate the eroding of borders. In a foreign land, it's normal to want comfort. In the evening, following an exhausting day of meetings, my colleague and I discovered ourselves in the city. It began as a casual bond and became more intense as we shared experiences from our lives outside the office. The different cultural backgrounds made it feel secluded and almost defiant as if the moments took place within a bubble separate from the real world. Reality, however, isn't going to stay in the shadows all the time.

When connections at work become personal, they often carry unintended consequences--jealousy, resentment, or infidelity. I've observed great people struggle with emotions they had no intention of acting on. "It just happened," they'd claim like they were being swept away by a wave they could not resist. But the truth is that the situations mentioned above don't "just happen." They're caused by moments when the boundaries were not acknowledged, and tiny choices grew into bigger ones.

The hurt isn't just restricted to the people directly affected. Whether physical or emotional, betrayal leaves a trail of pain, not only in romantic relationships but also within the workplace. The team's trust is broken; they fail, and the people affected often bear the burden of their regrets for a long time after the initial attraction has faded. This human battle reminds me of the expression, "Boundaries are not just about keeping others out; they're about keeping yourself in."

Then, what's the best solution? What can we do to honour the bonds that make our workplace more intimate while safeguarding the integrity of our personal lives and relationships? The answer is in being intentional. The first step is to identify when the bonds of professional relationships are crossing into personal boundaries and stop to think about what we pay for going over this boundary.

Self-awareness and open communication: Self-awareness and open communication are vital. You are allowed to feel emotions but avoid acting on these feelings in ways that may hurt yourself or others. When it comes to professional relationships, establishing a relationship before the start can help avoid confusion in the future. Don't be too confident, in particular, when power dynamics are in place. If you're in an uncomfortable circumstance, don't be afraid to ask for advice from your mentor, HR, or another trusted third party.

The most important thing is to stay focused on your beliefs. It should be where we can help each other, not where we become lost. I once heard, *"You can't build trust in one place by breaking it in another."* The paradox of professional life is always there; however, how we deal with it is entirely within our reach. Through awareness, honesty, and integrity, we can build connections that enrich our lives without jeopardizing the integrity of those connections.

The Role of Power and Authority in Romantic Entanglements

Within the intricate web of workplace life, power and authority can shift the lines between coworkers and create surprising romantic connections. The dynamic could seem exciting and unstable, usually driven by the enticement of power and authority that those in control tend to exhibit. *"Attraction to power,"* the experts say, isn't only related to the power position but instead the persona, the sense of direction or determination that makes people feel enticed to seek the comfort of someone who can command the space. However, the dance starts with this attraction and must be handled carefully to avoid stumbling.

Realities of Professional Life

I recall the times when I felt unintentionally drawn to a person working. The reason was not just their job title; it was their self-confidence, how they conducted their bodies, and how they could control a space with their charisma. *"Power isn't just held; it's worn,"* I have read. They carried it as an extra skin. It was a sultry scent. However, beneath it lay something I was not prepared for.

It began as a primary exchange but quickly grew into an important thing. Every feedback session increased in intensity, and each glance exchanged was important. Then, all the excitement turned into a cloud of dread. *"Am I seen differently now?"* I want to consider it. Did anyone in the team notice this? Could it be because they were in the process of judging? The whispers that echoed throughout the hallways were not simply the result of a nightmare.

The other day, I was listening to an exchange that was more stinging than I anticipated. *"It's obvious why they got the project,"* somebody told me. I stopped. Did my value as a professional decrease due to this relationship? No matter how unintentional, the act of favouritism is a sign of betrayal for anyone left behind. Then came the shame- was I also infringing on their professional development? The power imbalance between us didn't only concern hierarchies; it was an invisible line that shifted that neither of us could manage.

It was a sour end if our relationship soured the way it often happens. Our meetings were tense, and our relationship as professionals weakened. I'd read that somewhere: "Romance in power is like dancing on thin ice; eventually, it cracks." The result was each of us struggling to preserve respect and dignity.

What is the lesson? Boundaries matter. An insightful moment came from a teacher who said, *"The head must guide where the heart dares to tread."* Transparency is essential, not just to each other, but to ourselves. The policies serve a purpose and offer the framework for protecting not just the careers of people but their psychological well-being.

My experience with the pain has shown me that although the power of power may be attractive, navigating through it takes determination to establish boundaries. If you don't, the dancing will only end in regret.

The Impact of Distance on Relationship Fidelity

It's exciting to travel for work, perhaps even addicting. The bustle and movement and the excitement of walking into new towns, breathing in new locations' fresh air, and knowing that you're making things occur. However, every journey is a reminder of what is happening and who remains at home. Each mile that passes between us tugs on something fragile. It is said that *"Absence makes the heart grow fonder,"* but if your absence extends into several weeks, it puts you to the test by stretching your heart and your trust in your loved one.

Realities of Professional Life

Working from home has an enticing appeal: the rhythm of airports and the challenges of emerging cities. However, every mile I travel is like a thread stretched thin, threatening to come undone. The saying goes, *"Distance makes the heart grow fonder,"* but the reality is more nuanced. Distance tests everything.

A few hours later, in the rooftop bar following an event, the city was sparkling under me as a coworker, and I laughed. It was only a momentary, innocuous memory to the naked eye but a long-lasting memory. The moment revealed a reality I was not ready to confront--loneliness creates an attraction. This isn't because the connection to home isn't vital. However, the proximity of those who know what you're going through may confuse you.

The trips shed a very harsh spotlight on minor imperfections in confidence. A long day can transform goodnight phone calls into chores, or sharing the boring, like how the taxi driver was overcharged, feels like a minor issue. However, it's not. Check-ins like these are essential. In the absence of them, the silence is loud. A friend once said, *"When you're gone, it's like living half a life."* This shattered something inside me. However, it also kept me awake.

The Distance creates vulnerability, which only honesty can counter. I've realized that "Today was lonely" or "I'm scared I'm missing too much." The honesty of this kind helps keep the relationship in place. It's a bridge based on mutual understanding and the realization that both sides are willing to sacrifice.

There's also the appeal of comfort. A smile from those who can understand is the comfort of a place that's not familiar. The risk of sacrificing the rest of your life for a short connection isn't worth it. To stop this from happening, my boundaries have been set with my partner: open conversations regarding who I'm spending the most time with, regular calls even when I'm exhausted in my sleep, and making sure I know why I'm at home.

Every flight back is an opportunity to reaffirm the strength. Distance-stretched relationships can end up breaking, or with intention and attention, they could grow. My personal goal is to prove that distances don't determine the love of a person. It's only a test of its power.

Balancing Career Ambitions with Personal Commitments

Achieving a balance between career goals and obligations is like a stable tightrope at one moment, sliding at the other. It's thrilling to chase your desires and attain the height of accomplishment in the workplace, where every move and success can be a significant step toward reaching your target. For families with a household member in the home, your path toward success will come with an expense. The cost is not noticed until it could end the very foundations of things that you hold as you most highly.

Realities of Professional Life

I still remember those late nights in hotels with no privacy between meetings. I remember the feeling of achievement tempered by the emptiness of silence that arose after I had stopped my movements. These were times when I'd look through the photos of my spouse and the lives we shared, being both intimate and disengaged. It was a routine to call home at first, with eager updates like vital messages shared. However, as workplace demands grew, calls became smaller and decreased frequently until silence took over the space in which laughter was once.

"Absence makes the heart grow fonder," it is said; however, too much of it leaves a gap that words cannot compensate for. There weren't any significant events that broke our bonds, but the small ones. The absence of a morning cup of coffee, laughter over dinner, or an intimate time spent with each other. The routines

we once had were shattered as I began to feel like I was a guest within my existence.

The most painful realization occurred in a social gathering with polished smiles and an easy camaraderie. I was having a laugh with a friend over a joke shared and feeling briefly it was like a dangerous feeling of a connection. This was nothing that I thought about, just a brief time. In my soul, however, I realized that this was a sign of caution that infidelity isn't an outright announcement. It begins as a twirl of a slight change in the loyalty of someone in the home when the relationship is stretched thin.

It was painful to realize this and forced me to face a brutal fact: ambition without balance can be a costly risk of losing someone you love. Then, I realized that love doesn't just have to be about extravagant gestures. It's all about deciding to keep in touch regardless of distance, which makes it difficult. The key is sending that image of your day, making the time to make a meaningful call or text, "I miss you," even when you're too exhausted to communicate.

The process of rebuilding was complex. It was about acknowledging my partner's sacrifices -- the hours they spent juggling every aspect on their own, the achievements I had missed. However, in the acknowledgement, the relationship changed. If I told them, "I see you, and I'm grateful," the response of "I'm proud of you" was our take-away.

We also set our boundaries, which included less travel when possible and plans for reunions that weren't only returns but also renewals. When I got home, it wasn't to my home but also to be reminded of the strength we'd developed. As a team, we discovered that ambition does not have to be a source of tension when approaching the challenge with purpose and integrity.

"Ambition demands a price," However, the relationship we nurtured has proven that through effort, commitment can stand up to the most challenging test. It is possible that distance could hinder affection, but it enhances it when both hearts decide to remain rooted in the path they travel together.

Work Cultural Influences on Work-Life Balance

When working in professions that require long hours and continuous availability are sought after, we typically adopt a mindset that encourages constant commitment. The phrases *"sleep is for the weak"* or *"the hustle never stops"* seem harmless enough, yet they could affect how our personal lives are viewed. If a person's professional life relies on sacrifice, typically, they carry that expectation into their home. If your work environment expects you to respond to emails late at night, the same habits will be reflected in how you talk to your spouse and family members. What after that? It could be anger, maybe even isolation. Every profession has its own set of pressures, and every culture affects its members through subtle means. When we understand this, we can make informed decisions to nurture our bonds with our loved ones rather than weaken these relationships. Keeping the delicate balance and creating the proper boundaries will protect the aspects of us that belong to us and the people we love. These are the ones that remain unaffected by the demands of work. It's not always easy, but by being honest and compassionate, you can navigate the interactions between work and personal life gracefully while protecting those most critical connections.

Realities of Professional Life

Workplace culture can be a quiet creator, shaping people's lives in ways we seldom consider. In the past, I was amid an occupation that required all of me - my time, attention, my rest. I took my work at home with me, not in files or laptops, but rather in the shape of expectations that increased daily. The thief was quiet and stole moments that weren't mine to forfeit. *"Success demands sacrifice,"* he claimed, yet no mention was made of the collateral harm.

Cracks started to appear within my marriage before I recognized him. My spouse, who was once my refuge, became an object of my desire. The late nights at work became missed meals and unread messages into mute anger. *"You're here, but you're not present,"* he spoke to me one evening, his voice cracking due to the burden of isolation. The words still echo throughout my thoughts. The neglect was not deliberate. However, it happened and left him feeling unnoticed.

Such habits are commonly seen in the fields where unwavering determination is prized. The tech industry I once thrived in is now based on quoting phrases like "The grind never stops." In my case, it didn't end, and it soaked into my family, my weekend schedule, and my relationships. My work culture made me determine my worth through efficiency, and I subsequently forgot what it meant to be present in the lives of the people I valued. The miniature disconnects started as a few missed discussions, unintentional nods, and an emotional chasm. Then, in the void of that emotional canyon, the vulnerability sank in.

The act of Infidelity doesn't have to be intended. Sometimes, it's urgent to connect when the relationships become too tense. In my case, it was watching the gradual unravelling of a lover who wanted my attention but was distracted enough not to notice. I remember his words: *"I don't feel like I matter to you anymore."* These words hurt, yet he revealed an aspect I was unprepared to accept. As he remained and cried, he took comfort from someone else's ability to listen, a relief I'd given up.

There's more than one field of work. One of my close friends in the healthcare field told her story of the same struggles. The nurse showed all her love to the patients and returned home empty-handed to her husband. She was exhausted and built walls that she hadn't planned to create. "It wasn't about not loving him," she told me. "It was about not having anything left to give." The person she was with found comfort through emotional connections elsewhere, not from desire, but rather out of a need.

It's happened to families with executives, as well. People juggling their work and pressures tend to forget the time alone they and their families crave. Children are taught to eat dinner alone, couples learn how to make up for silences independently, and eventually, disconnection develops. When this happens, Infidelity isn't a cause of the relationship's failure; it's just the result of the absence of emotional connection that isn't addressed.

However, I've also witnessed some hope in my own experience. The first step is to acknowledge the problem out loud. My partner and I sat down to discuss the truths we'd hidden under the pretence of "just being busy." This wasn't an easy task. However, it was essential. Small rituals were created. Sunday nights were our times for conversation and to re-align. We named it the "reset button," a place to talk about our feelings or share happiness and listen.

I've learned that boundaries aren't only related to work. He's all about respect - for your spouse, yourself, and your relationship. I was unable to answer emails after that time. I took my mobile in the bedroom. It was a small thing, but it made a fortress of the areas of my life that were most important to me. One of my mentors once said, *"Boundaries aren't walls; they're doors you choose to open and close."* This is something I do daily, consciously.

Empathy is the second part of the puzzle. The workplace is challenging, but understanding each other's needs could help create bridges instead of walls. Once we stopped blaming each other for a time we didn't get, we began appreciating those moments we could share.

In retrospect, I realize the importance of work and how it doesn't need to be the sole focus of your life. What we learn from our work doesn't need to determine how we feel or feel connected. This is a lesson that I've learned in the past, but one I hold very close. Like everything worth developing, take dedication, trust, and the strength to defend the most important things to you.

Here's what I'd tell anyone struggling with this stress to do: Stop. Reflect. Consider what I am willing to risk. Then fight for those parts in your existence that are yours to cherish--not just as a job but as someone who cares, loves, and is loved back. The goal isn't perfection; it's about being present. There's no time to take a different path.

Urban Entanglements

The cityscapes reveal a paradox in human life: They beckon us to connect but challenge us by weighing down the disconnection. Imagine yourself walking down a busy street where faces surround you. The gazes of each person flicker for a brief moment before they drift away unnoticed. The city is both magical and cursed by its ability to be everywhere and nowhere simultaneously and to enjoy anonymity while grappling with its silence. *We are invited to tell our stories in the city, but this is often done at the expense of real belonging.*

In the midst of pulsating traffic and towering skyscrapers, schedules dictate a constant rhythm in relationships. The noise, the distractions and the demands in an environment which never rests must be endured. Urban life offers many opportunities for growth and success but also fragments time. This leaves little room for meaningful connections. Intimacy can be lost in the rush of deadlines, even if partners try hard to hang on. Relationships are stretched in the city, and their endurance is tested.

Even the most lively of social interactions can be tainted by loneliness. It's cruel to be alone in a crowd. Every fleeting connection--a hurried handshake or a casual conversation-- reminds one of what could be, yet rarely is. In a busy cafe, patrons often have their heads down and focus on screens rather than the people around them. Forming bonds in such an environment is a conscious act that requires a lot of courage.

Then, there is the complex of cultural collisions. The cities are melting pots where different cultures converge and create friction. Lover may have to navigate their history, belief, and dream intersections. Diversity is both a blessing and a problem, requiring empathy and flexibility in equal measures. *Love and friendship can grow unexpectedly in these places, requiring resilience to overcome the underlying undercurrent of misunderstanding.*

In the midst of all this, city life teaches us one important truth: Sanctuary is created by you. Intimacy thrives in places where there is intention, whether it's shared rituals or quiet corners. This is about creating oases in the chaos and finding rhythm within a constantly moving world. The essence of urban relationships is seen in this pursuit. It's not about resisting city pulls but choosing what anchors you in its current.

The Role of Nightlife and Entertainment in Fostering Connections

As the city's pulse changes with the sunset, something awe-inspiring occurs. The spaces that are buzzing with daily activity transform into centres of possibilities, where exciting experiences are just as frequent as flickering light. In these dimly lit areas, such as buzzing bars and more tranquil Jazz clubs, subtle laws of daylight are loosened. People are relaxed, more courageous, and drawn towards connections. The night encourages people to share a laugh, a song they love, or an ongoing discussion.

Stories of Urban Life

Night has always had a unique appeal for me. Its rhythms are distinctive and almost hypnotic. They draw individuals into a dance of potential. I've witnessed the transformation of cities when the sun sets under the city's horizon. The streets that once were familiar are filled with laughter, music, and that quaint noise of hope.

The other night, I discovered myself in a darkly illuminated lounge, surrounded by strangers, yet somehow feeling connected. A soft tune played in the background, and the two of us smiled over the top of our glasses. "Sometimes," I thought, "all it takes is a moment for curiosity to spark." Conversations briskly flowed, after which, for a short time, it was as if we'd become acquaintances. Then, the change occurred--a subdued reminder of where these pathways could take us.

The nightlife scene is, despite its charm, a tricky path. This freedom can tempt us even when we feel dull or uneasy at home. I've seen this unfold as well. Minor indiscretions begin as innocent laughter that a stranger shares but then turn into a big problem. "Infidelity," a friend confessed once, "doesn't start in the heart; it starts in the mind--when you tell yourself it's harmless." Even though nightlife does not cause sexual infidelity, it can provide an environment where the temptation may be accurate.

The answer isn't just to stay out of the evening and take it in stride. It's all about honesty and boundaries. In my experience, being honest with your spouse about your plans for social life can go a long way. Also, remaining aware of what you value and most will act as a guide when you're on the go. "Connection thrives where there's trust," I once heard someone tell me. And they had a point.

It's not only about safeguarding relationships; it's seeking genuine connections in the short time that nightlife provides. Look for conversations that stay with you, not just those that are entertaining. Be around people who can inspire and lift you even when the music is loud and the lighting is dim.

The nightlife mirrors what we are looking for. When approached with a clear mind and intent, it transforms into an opportunity for connecting as well as a place for sharing pleasure and not for regret. It is all about recognizing its potential and following its path carefully. *"The night," I keep in mind, "is what you make out of it. Be wise in your choices."*

Navigating the Complex Web of City Relationships

In cities, people can slip by the masses like the cloak of anonymity. It's a feeling of freedom that comes with it- an ability to reinvent yourself with each new day and discover diverse versions of yourself within myriad settings. However, there's also a price to pay: the feeling of loneliness of being a stranger amid millions. Cities have a distinct advantage. On one hand, you can dream, create, and create relationships with no concern for their past names. However, on the flip side, the perpetual threat of secrecy could cause alienation, which keeps people moving through life without the possibility of a meaningful and lasting relationship.

Stories of Urban Life

I remember when the city initially felt like a getaway, an opportunity to resettle. In this city, nobody knew my history, and I was able to revel in this solitude. Every dawn promised a new beginning, and every sunset spoke stories of fulfilled dreams. However, as the years progressed, I realized this freedom's costs. I felt like a stranger to people who I saw daily. The faces blurred to the sea of silence. My closest friends were distant, like ships that passed by in the dark.

"Time and intimacy in a city are rarities; they're luxuries not easily afforded." The words shook me when I saw my friends' relationships deteriorate because of the burden of a busy calendar and endless interruptions. I witnessed couples who were previously in a constant struggle to get any time for one another. Meetings or deadlines and late-night phone calls

destroyed the foundation of their relationship. It's a city that doesn't pause and isn't slow enough to allow love to catch its breath.

Stress from financial problems only exacerbated the tension. Living expenses that were high made simple pleasures seem like stressors. Night outs with friends turned into budgeting. Surprise gifts were more of an indulgence rather than a gesture of affection. Many felt the pressure to keep a façade of achievement trumped the intimateness of sharing struggle. I watched the raging of arguments focusing on money but getting into deeper emotions. *"The urban struggle for financial stability reveals deeper emotional fault lines,"* one of my friends recently told me. I couldn't be more in agreement.

And then there's the problem of closeness. When you live in a city, you are immersed in the city, but it's not uncommon to feel totally in your world. I experienced it firsthand--navigating crowded subways, brushing past strangers, yet yearning for connection. It was easy to connect with strangers, yet it was hard to communicate with the people you met. My relationships were often merely transactional, just like a few moments spent in the dim light of a neon, not to be re-visited. Although it was liberating, the anonymity was challenging to be grounded in anything tangible. It was a constant cycle of friends that made me yearn for something more profound and more lasting.

Technology has added yet another level of complexity. Today, the internet is a mere swipe away. But that speed can lead to a sense of disconnection. I was browsing through profiles, enthralled by strangers' lives and ignoring the one beside me. It's simple to cover yourself behind screens and make two separate lives - one visible while the other is hidden. I've witnessed this duality in relationships, for example, receiving a message from a stranger when sitting with a friend or a conversation interrupted due to the compulsion of a notification. It was easy for technology's ease to discover new connections; however, it also created a gap between the current and the reality.

The city's beauty is its diversity. However, diversity could cause tension in relationships. I have a friend with a culture that is vastly different from my own. It was at first exciting to experience the world from a different angle. As time progressed, the differences became obvious—the expectations of family members vying with individual desires. Daily routines became conflicts. It requires patience and openness to reach a compromise. *"The beauty of diversity lies in its capacity to broaden perspectives, yet it requires patience and compromise,"* I tried to remind myself of that, and somehow, we were able to overcome these difficulties.

What is the best way to get through these tangled urban landscapes? How can we avoid the lure of anonymity, financial pressure, and the distractions brought by technological advancement? It's been my experience that introspection is key. Connections in cities require an effort to be deliberate and an option to focus on connection in the chaos.

1. Moments of meaningful significance are the ones that provide a sense of security. I've witnessed couples flourish by creating rituals, such as morning coffee with each other, a solitary dinner, or a shared pastime. Small acts of kindness become holy, reminding us that even amid a hectic schedule, it's never too late for a moment of reconnection.
2. A city full of possibilities to explore. Some of my most cherished memories are of spontaneous adventures-- stumbling upon a hidden bookstore, discovering a quaint cafe, or simply walking through a vibrant

neighbourhood. These moments bring a sense of "us" that withstands the urban's ebb and flow.

3. An ensconced home can be an oasis. The house doesn't have to be lavish. It just has to appear like it's yours. I felt a sense of peace when creating a space that fits my character, a place that allowed me to relax and re-energize. In the case of relationships, this space serves as a base that is a sanctuary where love can be free from distractions in the world.

4. One of my best decisions was limiting how much screen time I spent during my time. If it's a rule of no phone at meals or a night without devices, these limits allow for genuine conversations and presence.

5. While cultural differences can be difficult, they are also beneficial. My experience has taught me that approaching the subject with curiosity instead of judgment can open the door to deeper understanding. There's no need to erase distinctions, but instead, it should be about making them a part of the celebration and discovering harmony among the differences.

The city, with its many facets, has taught me to value the depth of my knowledge over its breadth. It's not just about how many individuals you've met but the depth to which you understand the people you know. Intimacy requires being vulnerable and willing to take a moment and be fully in the moment. I've come to appreciate the rare moments when masks disappear while the city's hum disappears in the distance.

The most successful relationships in the city are based on honesty and the willingness to come to your true self despite the city's many opportunities to conceal. It's a delicate balance that requires effort but can be a huge reward. When everything changes, individuals who take a moment to contemplate and live in the moment will discover that genuine relationships aren't just feasible but deeply rewarding.

Allure of Attraction

Attraction's enticement is as long-lasting as streams that cut their way through the ancient valleys. Attraction is like the stars above weaving through the web of human connections. Attraction isn't just an urge but an orchestra of individual, cultural, and ecological notes played incredibly harmoniously. It is necessary to look past the surface to explore the complex environmental model and fully understand what it is. This structure is as complex and interconnected as the ecosystems that support life.

Imagine a beautiful forest at sunrise in which every part is connected. The trees extend out their arms towards the sky, and the leaves whisper to the wind; the roots reach into the fertile soil. In the same way, our relationships with others can be influenced by the interaction of individual characteristics as well as our surroundings. The model of ecological attraction shows us that our wants do not come from a singular source. They are intertwined in the various layers that surround us, including our culture, society, and personal experiences.

Physical attractiveness, along with its irresistible appeal, can be described as the vibrant flower of a wildflower called a bee. It's a force that creates intimacy and passion. However, as a philosophy of Friedrich Nietzsche observed, *"All great things must first wear terrifying and monstrous masks. "* The attraction is captivating but can be a sign of weakness within relationships. If you are faced with the lure of choosing a more appealing option, it could undermine the strength of commitment and the strength of the emotional bonds.

The ecological model requires the reader to think about deeper issues. What draws us to particular types of beauty? How does the society in which we reside increase or diminish these appeals? This model suggests that just as the bird's song is affected by the habitat that it resides in, decisions are influenced by the intangible and often invisible nature of our surroundings.

Through this investigation, we discover that the feelings of discontent and unhappiness do not just reflect a failure from the heart but are reflections of unmet demands and environmental influences. They remind us that love, as nature, thrives most effectively when balanced. Maybe it's in being aware of the forces at play that help us to build relationships, recognizing beauty not only for its fleeting radiance but also as a greater understanding of life's huge and connected web of life.

Understanding Personal Stimulus Characteristics

Personality-related stimuli are inherent aspects that may trigger a response from other people. For romantic situations, they are things like body appearance and skin colour, which are frequently perceived subconsciously but significantly impact attraction between people.

Navigating Reality

It was late at night when I began browsing my phone for hours. Seeing a photo of him with a different person with eyes that sparkled with love was painfully sad. "How could this happen?" I thought as tears came to my eyes. In my soul, I realized that it wasn't only about the love affair and the fling; it was about those hidden connections that slowly broke us up.

Physical beauty is attractive. His eyes displayed a lustre, and that lured me when we first made contact. He frequently praised how my complexion "glowed in the sunlight." However, as time passed, it became apparent that his eyes started to drift, and he became attracted to characteristics I did not possess. It was clear that he was subject to the influence of society, and beauty and colour can be a factor in determining how we view ourselves.

The truth is that infidelity tends to thrive in insecure, unaddressed feelings. Later, he admitted, "It wasn't just her looks, but how she made me feel noticed, appreciated." The comments irritated me but highlighted our shared apathy about our previously cherished relationship.

We must take on these issues head-on to restore our confidence in ourselves. We sought counselling, which revealed the individual causes of how he behaved. *"Understanding isn't excusing,"* our counsellor clarified, "but it's the first step toward healing." Together, we focused on open dialogue in which we acknowledged and appreciated the importance of each other beyond the superficial aspects.

It was not just about forgiveness but also about discovering why we became drawn to each other. Looking back at our recent past, I hope different people learn from our experiences, recognize the subtle forces in relationships, and nurture them with love and awareness.

Social and Cultural Influences

The ecological model focuses on personal characteristics are essential, they cannot occur in isolation. The social norms, values of culture, and representations can influence what's considered appealing or desirable. The external influences provide a setting that places certain qualities above others, influencing individual decisions about partners.

Navigating Reality

I can remember sitting on the end of my bed, staring at my smartphone's screen glare while scrolling endlessly through photos of perfectly posed couples with smiling, airbrushed faces. *"Why don't we feel like that anymore?"* I wandered into the space. The media's depiction of perfect relationships and perfect relationships was also the persistent cultural whispers that celebrated the power of novelty over time and began to saturate my thoughts.

There wasn't always a time like this. At first, we loved our quirks, joining like pieces of a piece. However, somewhere in the process, a subtle appeal to acceptance by others began to creep in. "You deserve excitement," it seemed that the universe was whispering. The lines blurred when a friend working with me began to share inside jokes and steal smiles. The love wasn't there; it wasn't even close, and there was interest. I sensed a risky sense of self-esteem in that brief moment of attention.

I wasn't aware of the extent to which the influence of society played into my life until I started to think about it. We live in a world based on expectations - the perfect quality standards for beauty and the lively seeking companions. The stories we hear about can take away from the beauty of our lives. My friend once advised me, *"Don't let fleeting distractions rob you of a love built on depth and history."* It stuck in my mind.

The moment of truth came during an open conversation that was racked with tears and vulnerability. *"Why did we stop being each other's refuge?"* I'd wondered. We began to work on reconnecting and reducing external sounds. Small rituals were created - breakfast, coffee dates, evenings with no phones, and letters dropped into one another's pockets. Gradually, I realized that love isn't a result of extravagant gestures but the constant determination to choose each other each day.

Recognizing that pressures from outside increase frustration is vital. Recovering from the brink requires more than reconnection. It required a conscious rejection of society's constant pursuit of excellence.

Skin Color and Physical Appearance

In the complex relationship between humans, a person's physical appearance often is a critical factor in how we interact and our emotions. Skin colour, an essential element of our human diversity, has been the topic of admiration and prejudgment. Within the context of attraction, it's an instant visual signal that triggers strong emotions. The ecological theory framework suggest that those responses have their roots in evolutionary psychology. In this context, particular traits have traditionally indicated health or genetic fitness. In particular, research has found that many people perceive particular skin colours as appealing due to the influence of culture or social standards. The perceptions of these people can significantly affect relationships and initial attraction and satisfaction in partnerships.

Navigating Reality

It started in the evening when the air was full of tension. "I just don't feel seen anymore," my partner stated, his voice strained with exhaustion. The statement irritated me more than it needed to. The comment forced me to face the unsettling fact that our relationship was fading, partly due to the external appearance that had been an unspoken enemy in our friendship.

A person's physical appearance can be a constant factor in relationships of today. When I was younger, I remember my partner looking at me with admiration. *"Your smile lights up the room,"* he commented, leaving me shocked and confident. However, as time passed, social expectations began to haunt us. Through the plethora of carefully curated pictures, social media created unrealistic images of beauty. Skin colour and symmetry were seen as the most important quality indicators. I was constantly asking myself, "Am I enough?"

There was more than me. My partner, too, suffered from insecurities hidden beneath his polished exterior. The quiet jealousy of his perfectly symmetrical skin features or flawless appearance displayed in public places turned into a silent barrier between us. Discontent turned into distracting us, and we both began to look for beauty in each other and not so much in one another. There was the possibility of infidelity as a snatched guest because the potential for temptation outside of our bonds was more tempting than confronting our shared fears.

Then, one night, the whole thing unravelled. The phone rang, and a message appeared on his phone. The conversation was akin to emotional betrayal. My heart ached. I confronted him, and he fell apart. "It wasn't about love," he said through his crying, "it was about feeling desired."

That was when I realized the solution did not have to be blame or shame. It was time to build the foundation of our relationship, and that meant discovering the worth of our relationship over and above the superficial. "Let's try again," I declared, my voice shaking in hope.

Together, we delved into the root of our fears. We established boundaries on social media usage and were committed to honest praise. "You are so much more than your appearance" became our daily motto. Also, we set aside some time for physical and emotional intimate relationships. We paid attention to our hygiene and rejoiced with small gestures. The cracks slowly began to get better.

My experience has taught me that even though physical beauty can be powerful, it's not the main focus of a love affair. A mutual effort to acknowledge the value of the beauty of each other's inside and out is what keeps affection from the temptation of infidelity.

Navigating Attraction in Modern Relationships

The current relationship landscape presents various issues where exposure to different aesthetic standards in media may increase insecurity or desire to be different. Knowing the characteristics of a person's stimulus helps individuals overcome these obstacles with greater consciousness. The study of skin colour and physical appearance explains why people may stray from appealing options if they believe their partner's attraction has diminished with the years. Couples will be able to develop a more profound knowledge and understanding of the things that matter beyond superficial attraction when they recognize these components.

Navigating Reality

In their most basic nature, the bonds of relationships can be described as delicate tapestries made through shared laughter, snorted thoughts, and the satisfaction of genuinely being recognized. However, even the strongest bonds may fail under the pressure of contemporary complexities. It was a lesson I had to learn by trial and error, in instances of doubt and pain of wondering if I had sufficient.

The conversation started with a smile. "You've got to meet this new colleague of mine," my partner had stated with excitement flashing through his eyes. The first time I saw her, I laughed at my initial scepticism. It was true that she was beautiful, appealing, and had the confidence of a natural. It was lovely and caused you to beg for your reflection.

I attempted to scrub it off. In the end, attraction is natural. As the days turned into weeks, minor issues began to build up. One glance here and there and there, or a reminder of her successes there. The voice that rang in my head became more pronounced. "Am I still enthralling the man? Do I have a normal look?"

Physical attraction is powerful. It ignites the sparks and draws two souls closer. It's when a smile can light up a space or in the enchanting charm of their laughter. However, beauty alone cannot support the weight of love that lasts long. It became clear when I watched our conversations become more strenuous. Each conversation felt like a silent exchange between me and me.

I looked at my companion's every move, absorbing too much into the casual comments. "She's so talented," one of him had stated. A harmless comment, perhaps. However, my low self-esteem seemed like an accusation against me. I fell into the trap of not being set through him, but my fears and anxieties, as well as the ferocious aesthetic standards we are surrounded by.

The thrill of novelty is intoxicating. The lure of the undiscovered could be enough to make even the staunchest of hearts shake. I noticed tiny changes in his attitude to look better dressed and how his eyes sparkled when he spoke about her thoughts. My mind was flooded with the worst-case scenario. Did I lose the man to someone else who appeared to have something I could not?

I questioned him one night. I sat in the dark, my voice shaking in anger and fear. "Do you find her more attractive than me?" The question was hanging over the room, heavy and threatening. The shock in his voice was real, and his words of reassurance. However, words alone weren't enough to heal the hurts I'd caused to me.

The human brain is an intricate thing. Sometimes, just the impression of an attraction fading can make someone fall for it. Although he didn't do any of it, I was aware of the possibility that circumstances might shift. The reason for infidelity is not necessarily affection or love; it's about feeling loved and appreciated or even escaping every day. "I've always been drawn to her energy," the man acknowledged in the course of a night. He wasn't confessing untruthfulness but rather an admission of the reality. At that point, I realized I didn't have to fight another woman. I was fighting the chasm that was growing between us.

We all knew that we had to be healed. We started by establishing the basic principles of honesty and communication. "What do you need from me to feel loved?" the man said. The question was simple; however, it triggered the doors to more conversations.

We started to re-discover the other in small steps each day. We had date nights when phones weren't allowed, lengthy walks during which we talked about our unspoken concerns, and moments in vulnerability that rekindled our feelings of connection. Also, I had to face my fears head-on and realize that my value wasn't determined in his eyes, nor anybody else's.

Over time, I realized that although attraction can be sparks, the emotional bond sustains the fire. The focus was on the most important: dreams shared of mutual respect and the pure happiness of sharing each other's space. I came to understand imperfections in beauty for him and me.

The answer to the problem of infidelity isn't the control of or monitoring--it's the knowing and working. By addressing the root causes--boredom, insecurity, or lack of communication--couples can strengthen their bond. In our case, this meant changing the definition of attraction by seeing our partners as whole persons rather than mere bodies or faces.

Infidelity or Reality

As I write this, I reflect on that time of turmoil and am grateful. It has taught me that relationships don't stay static. They change with time and require care and concern. As my friend once stated in our late-night discussions, "It's not about finding an individual who is better than you. It's about building a stronger relationship."

What's the point of love? Choosing to be with each other regardless of flaws or imperfections every day.

A Framework for Understanding Attraction

The ecosystem-based model offers an entire framework to examine how personal factors like skin colour and physical appearance affect our behaviour when it comes to romantic situations. These are not passive characteristics; they serve as urgent stimuli which can cause profound reactions in others. Based on this theory, it is evident that people naturally gravitate to those with specific desirable characteristics. The attraction to attractive features is rooted in evolutionary biology. Physical attributes often signify fertility, health, and genetic fit. In turn, these characteristics are a significant indicator of relationship fidelity and satisfaction.

Navigating Reality

"Sometimes, I find myself reminiscing about the intricate layers of love and attraction and how they interweave into our relationships like a double-edged sword. Love is beautiful, but oh, the lure of attraction--it's a force of nature. I've learned this lesson the hard way."

The whole thing began with the golden light of summer. My spouse and I were both in the honeymoon stage. Each glance seemed electric; each touch emitted vows too precious to speak. In every way, it is an ideal illustration of the power of passion. However, as time went by, cracks started to appear. This was not due to a lack of affection but due to the pressure of daily life diminished passion.

I ran into someone at an office conference a few days ago. Let's call the person "the magnet." The magnet was not spectacular, but his character and the city were captivating. His laughing was infectious, his self-confidence was unshakeable, and his interest in my thoughts was enthralling. I was drawn to him not because I was apathetic but because the attraction seemed to ignite an unused part within me.

"Why does this happen?" I was able to recall asking myself this question while overwhelmed by guilt but filled with excitement from the illicit. That's when the ecological Model of Attraction is a way to comprehend why we feel how we feel even when we do not want to.

The ecological model states how physical appearance, charm, or common interests function like "urgent stimuli." The magnet's attraction and sensitivity towards particulars became beacons and led me to magnets. The evolution of biology is just one of the reasons. Humans can recognize signals of energy, intelligence, and speaking ability. This isn't just a matter of the appearance of our skin, but it is functional. It's about those subtle characteristics that link with us emotionally.

In this case, the attraction's physical gestures, their smiling posture, and the way their eyes puckered when they smiled all came together, creating an impossible attraction to resist. This is the exact way that the specific hue of blue could attract the artist during a sunset. There is no rational explanation for it. It's just an unavoidable draw.

However, here's the problem with attraction: it's not a separate entity. It's a challenge to the core values of commitment, faith, and love. If those foundations start to shake, even a little, the compulsion to be "the other" grows stronger.

In retrospect, my vulnerability wasn't rooted in discontent with my spouse but rather a desire to be seen indeed. It wasn't the gap my partner had left; they had a desire I hadn't realized I felt. However, for other people, there's an entirely different tale. The degree of satisfaction in relationships--or lack of it is an effective indicator of fidelity. When we feel dissatisfied, ignoring or dismissing the attraction to being a stranger becomes a method to feel validated.

I can remember reading about how the presence of a gorgeous person can increase confidence in yourself due to social validation. While my spouse and I were always attractive in our writing, with compliments from people we know and love enhancing the "picture-perfect" dynamic--it wasn't enough to protect us from the nefarious effects of temptations from outside.

The temptation can come unexpectedly, like a stealer at night. It does not announce itself via the sound of a trumpet but instead slowly creeps into the room, wrapped with informal conversations and innocent smiles.

In the beginning, I shared secret things with the magnet. It was initially trivial, such as my favourite songs or embarrassing tales. Then, the conversations were more personal. The attraction caused me to feel alive in an experience that was simultaneously exhilarating and scary.

The issue wasn't that they were "better" than my partner. The problem was the way their creativity made the every day seem excellent. The ecological model clearly describes the phenomenon: Third-party attractiveness creates a dissonance in the brain, a battle between our current situation and what we want. This isn't just about appearances but also timing, personal characteristics, and occasional sheer luck.

In one instance, in a vulnerable time, my magnet congratulated me on something my spouse had been unaware of for several years. The single compliment carries such a weight that it almost ended my engagement.

"How could I?" I asked myself over and over. I was feeling numb. However, the urge was as strong as the scent of perfume on an old jacket. It was clear that I had to choose; however, I must understand the root of my emotions before deciding.

I struggled with the internal struggle of wanting the magnet but knowing that my affection for my spouse was not fading. Minds are powerful rationalizers. Mine tried to convince me that my emotions were not harmful and weren't a sign of the slightest bit of betrayal. But deep down, I knew better.

The immediate pleasure of being in the vicinity of a magnet was more important than my goals for the future. Their laughter and their presence were relentless but short-lived.

After I confessed my feelings to my spouse, I expected an outburst of anger. But what I received instead was an intense sadness that shattered my heart. It also served as a turning point, a chance to revive what we'd nearly lost.

1. My companion and I began talking openly, without filtering regarding our desires, fears, and anxieties. The process wasn't simple--opening up seldom isn't--but it proved to be the foundation of our healing. I shared with them about the magnet, but not in detail; however, it was enough to share my thoughts without inflicting excessive pain.

2. It was clear that the physical bond, although important, was not enough to last us. We began doing activities together, strengthening our bond: reading books,

cooking, and reminiscing about places that held memories.

3. It was probably the most difficult to accept that being attracted is an inherent element of our human being. After we stopped discussing it as a negative, the issue could be addressed without shame or guilt. In one instance, my friend confessed that they'd felt the same attraction to someone else but decided to put their needs ahead of the two of us. This helped me feel less lonely and more confident in my dedication.

It's been a long time since I lived that particular chapter of my story, and even though the attraction is in the past, the lessons they accidentally taught me are still vivid memories. The path to love isn't straight-lined. It's an arduous road full of detours, pitfalls and distractions. However, at the core, it's a decision.

I picked my spouse. I try to pick the person I want to be with daily. It's not because the temptation has disappeared, and our relationship is more vital than a temporary enticement.

The ecological model suggests attraction is inevitable. But it is also a matter of resilience. When we understand the factors that shape us and fight them head-on, we build relationships that can withstand even the harshest weather.

"Love," as someone wise once said, "isn't about finding someone perfectly. It's about understanding imperfections and people perfectly." No magnetic force could keep you from your love when you've done that.

Philosophical Perspectives on Attraction and Infidelity

The lure of attraction is a long-standing study area in the philosophy of mind because it reveals the core of human desires and the dynamic of relationships. Philosophical theories can aid in our knowledge of why people may get drawn towards infidelity when confronted with appealing alternatives, specifically when viewed through the prism of an ecological framework.

Navigating Reality

I've been at the intersection of passion and dedication, battling the weight of decisions that sometimes seemed too much to take on. It's strange. How a smile, glance, or even an accidental stroke of the hand could trigger feelings to the point that one questions the foundation of your existence. However, attraction can be like fire and make you feel warm or consume you entirely according to how you handle fire.

In the past, I believed I was a lover. It wasn't until I experienced a sense of attraction to someone not in my circle of friends that I realized the extent of its complexities. Attraction, according to Plato, has once believed it, is a force that attracts us. It draws us to things we believe to be attractive, usually overriding our rational minds. I experienced this when I encountered someone who seemed so easy; it surprised me.

"It's just admiration," I told myself. If it's not controlled, admiration could turn into something more dangerous.

Modern living has a method that tests even the firmest obligations. Social media, for example, is a showcase of perfection curated by a curator, swarming users with pictures of the impossible but seemingly within our reach. This is how it began for me. It was a text message, a comment, and an idea of something harmless that became something I was unable to avoid.

The ecological model describes the phenomenon in detail. A person's physical appearance, mannerisms, and even the timbre of one's voice could trigger a response immediately. I was drawn to this particular person, not just because they were more attractive than my friend, but because they represented a different kind of happiness, a way to gain acceptance.

When I was in more tranquil moments, my thoughts were echoed by my thoughts of Kantian notions of the obligation of loyalty and fidelity. "Am I betraying the trust of someone who loves me unconditionally?" I pondered in my head. It's more than just a matter of lying. It's a crime of deceit and a sabotage of the moral foundation that creates bonds between people. However, I was caught in a web of conflicting feelings: loyalty, love, vitality, and stability.

A few nights ago, I looked at my reflection and cried across my face. "What am I doing?" I asked myself. What we choose to do during these times determines our relationships and identity.

Sartre was the one who provided me with the knowledge to see how to follow. Sure, I was enslaved by my desires, like I was in no control over my choices. The existentialist viewpoint of Sartre taught me that freedom isn't just simply about having no temptations; it's about choosing it. While it's possible to be tempted by instinct, you can choose to do fidelity. The consequences of choices are a lot more severe.

The lure of escape may be captivating, especially when a relationship is rough. However, love doesn't mean avoiding problems; it's about facing the storm with one another. I started asking myself the tough questions: what did I want in this relationship that I was not finding within my relationships? Was it possible to address these needs within the marriage I committed to?

The moment of truth came when I spoke out about my feelings. However, not to the person I had been but to my spouse. "I feel distant," I acknowledged. This wasn't an easy thing to do to admit, but it was sincere. We worked together to rekindle the bond that had weakened over time. We reviewed shared hopes, explored new ones, and found ways to ignite the spark that first brought us closer to one another.

Additionally, I was able to see beauty and not attach it. Being awed by someone's charm or intelligence does not have to result in being a victim. Much like art at a gallery, it can be viewed and enjoyed without having to be taken into the home.

Infidelity, as a fundamental, can be a sign of more significant issues, whether within us or in our relationships. When we address these root causes and address the root causes, we can turn moments of temptation into occasions to grow. It's not about perfect; it's about endurance. It would help to choose someone who understands your lowest and believes in you at your best.

If you're standing in the same spot I was and feeling the tug of temptation and the burden of guilt, be aware that you're not the only one. While the road ahead could be difficult, it can also be rewarding. "We are our choices," according to Sartre stated. Take your time and make wise decisions.

Navigating Romantic Relationships

Regarding romance, moral considerations are often the primary compass in our actions and decisions. What we choose to do when we are in love isn't just individual; it affects our lives and the quality of our relationships, emotional well-being, and psychological well-being. Philosophical theories like deontology, utilitarianism, and virtue ethics offer a framework for comprehending these complicated interactions.

Navigating Reality

"Sometimes, the lines blur," I thought, looking out the window to watch rain splash through the window. It was a relatively silent evening that made you feel as if my thoughts drifted into a moment when I was at an intersection of duty and desire. In all their complexity, relations are an oasis and a combat zone. My own story, along with many others, was formed by the choices we make, our emotions, and the moral frameworks guiding our lives.

It started innocently. An unintentional chat in the work breakroom was transformed into conversations that felt...different. There was a lot of laughter, understanding, and a feeling of connection that I didn't realize I had missed. "It's just a harmless friendship," I told myself, ignoring my growing anxiety when I spotted the man.

But deep down, I knew I was treading dangerous waters. Love's ethics, according to philosophers such as Aristotle and Kant would argue, require the highest level of integrity and commitment. However, according to what a useful could suggest, I started justifying my choices with thoughts such as, "If this connection makes me happy and doesn't hurt anyone, isn't that okay? "

This wasn't a good idea. I had been telling myself lies. My situation became painfully obvious one night when my spouse asked me, "Is everything alright between us? You've seemed distant." His words hit me with the force of a lightning bolt. Trust, the foundational element of our bond, was getting frayed as I was the one who pulled the strings.

As I look back, I realize how philosophical concepts regarding ethics can be applied to my situation:

I justified my growing love by weighing the joy against potential damage. This calculation, however, was flawed since I was not aware of the harm that my infidelity to me would bring.

Based on deontological ethics, it is an unalterable and indefinite moral obligation. It was a nagging thought since I realized I was violating a commitment my friend had believed in.

This person's perspective raised a new issue: What kind of individual do I wish to become? My actions didn't represent the honest and trustworthy friend I had hoped to become.

These theories gave me a framework to see my struggle; however, implementing the solution was different.

A few days ago, when I was sharing coffee with a colleague, He casually said, "You deserve to feel happy and appreciated." This thought echoed through my head for a long time. The words weren't the only thing that reverberated in my mind that reaffirmed me; it was the confirmation I sought. While it smacked my ego, it also revealed that my frustration wasn't with his character; it was a reflection of the gap in my emotional relationship with my spouse.

In the evening, I came to the choice. It was the right time to confront the growing gap in my life, not seek refuge elsewhere. It was raw, emotional, and complex. "I feel like we've drifted apart," I said to my companion, crying. "And I think I've been looking for connection in the wrong places."

He didn't respond angrily; however, it was a silent heartbreak. "Why didn't you tell me sooner?" the man said, his voice filled with regret.

Rebuilding trust after infidelity--emotional or physical--is akin to repairing a shattered vase. There are pieces, but there are cracks. The way we began our complex process

The first step was to be honest by laying everything on the table. "What do you need from me to feel secure again?" the man said. He asked a question that was easy yet profound in its compassion.

The decision to seek professional assistance was a significant turning point. The therapist we worked with guided us through difficult conversations, assisting us to identify the root causes we hadn't dealt with. She helped us understand ideas such as actively listening and the concept of emotional attunement, which helped us strengthen our bonds.

I cut ties with my colleague, not because he was wrong for me, but because it was not a good fit for my beliefs and values. It wasn't concerned with respecting my friend and coworker; it was about respecting me.

It takes time to build trust. There were instances when doubts emerged, and I had to demonstrate my faith by taking consistent action. "I'm not perfect," I remarked to him, "but I'm trying every day to be better."

My experiences taught me the art of balancing individual desires and ethical responsibilities. Attraction, as our therapist described it, is regular and doesn't necessarily indicate that you've let your lover down. It's what you do with these thoughts.

The most important thing isn't instant gratification but rather long-term harmony. I chose to place my love for someone else over a fleeting emotion by this concept.

The principle of integrity became my guideline--an obligation that I did not owe to my wife but to myself as an individual of honesty.

Cultivating virtues such as honesty and self-awareness transformed how I thought about love and commitment.

Physical or emotional infidelity can be a sign of physical or emotional infidelity and not a sign of illness. It is a sign of unfulfilled requirements, conflicts that are not resolved, or personal fears. The following are some of the critical lessons I learned from my experience:

Know your motives. Are you looking for fulfilment, thrill, or escape? Look at the root of the issue instead of acting on impulse.

Please discuss your feelings with your partner before they escalate. Being vulnerable can help strengthen relationships.

Counselling and therapy may provide ways to deal with emotional issues.

It's not just about physical exclusivity. It's about respect and emotional love.

My partner and I are as strong as ever before, not because of avoiding mistakes but because we confronted these challenges head-on. "I love you," the man said one night when we watched the sunset. "Not for being perfect, but for being real."

It's not about never failing but about selecting each other every day and through daily life's chaos and confusion, Which is why I'm very grateful.

About The Author

Sweta Leena Panda is a versatile author, product marketer, and project manager who began writing professionally in 2012. Known for her storytelling infused with Real World experiences as a social worker, entrepreneur, and avid traveller, Sweta has published two books on **Kindle** and her recent paperback, **Mirage of Memories** and **Infidelity or Reality (Vol. I & II)** released in 2024 through Notion Press. Her upcoming novels - Life of a Loser, and How I Met Your Father—highlight her creative range and ability to connect with readers across diverse themes.

www.ingramcontent.com/pod-product-compliance
Lightning Source LLC
Chambersburg PA
CBHW021529150726
47990CB00006B/2160